THE TURKS AND CAICOS ISLANDS

Beautiful by Nature

Julia & Phil Davies

CARIBBEAN

Macmillan Education
Between Towns Road, Oxford OX4 3PP
A division of Macmillan Publishers Limited
Companies and representatives throughout the world

www.macmillan-caribbean.com

ISBN 978 0 333 77547 9

Colour separation by Tenon & Polert Colour Scanning Ltd

All photographs are copyright of the author

Printed in Malaysia

2010 2009 2008
13 12 11 10 9 8 7 6

A catalogue record for this book is available from the
British Library.

All photographs are copyright of the author.

TABLE OF CONTENTS

The Turks & Caicos Islands

Dry Land   **Tidal Flats**

1 Yankee Town
2 Chalk Sound
3 Cheshire Hall
4 Grace Bay
5 The Hole
6 Fort George Cay
7 Wades Green

8 Flamingo Pond
9 Conch Bar Caves
10 Middleton Cay
11 The Boiling Hole
12 Penniston Cay
13 Gibbs Cay
14 Pear Cay

0   5   10   Miles

North Caicos

Whitby

Parrot Cay

Dellis Cay

7   8

Kew

Providenciales

Pine Cay

6

Bottle Creek

Water Cay

North West Point

Little Water Cay

Donna Cay

Middle Caicos

Bambarra

Blue Hills

4

Conch Bar

9

3

The Bight

2

5

Lorimers

Five Cays

East Caicos

Man O' War Bush

Ocean Hole

West Caicos

1

Lake Catherine

Molasses Reef Wreck

Plandon Cay

French Cay

Bell Sound

Cockburn Harbour

11

South Caicos

Caicos Bank

10

Long Cay

Six Hill Cays

Grand Turk

Cockburn Town

13

Long Cay

West Sand Spit

12

Cotton Cay

14

Fish Cays

East Cay

Balfour Town

Little Ambergris Cay

Salt Cay

Big Ambergris Cay

N

Seal Cays

Bush Cay

Big Sand Cay

Turks Bank

HMS Endymion Wreck

CHAPTER ONE

Tranquil Turquoise Seas

Limestone Foundations

For the majority of visitors to the Turks & Caicos, their first sight is an aerial view, and from this lofty vantage all will agree that the most striking feature of this little-known island group must surely be the beautiful turquoise of the surrounding seas. Accentuated by the bright sunlight, this vibrant colour is offset by the moody blue of the open ocean in which this small nation resides. Perhaps surprisingly, this darker shade signifies the low levels of nutrients and microscopic organisms present, a common feature of tropical oceanic waters. Nonetheless, the contrasting blue-green waters that skirt the coasts are home to myriad organisms that teem within the celebrated coral reef gardens. From the air, waves may be seen buffeting the north and eastern shores, or forming a rim of white as they break over the shallow reefs that fringe the islands. But, far from destroying the coastline, the sea and its inhabitants have formed, then shaped and moulded the whole archipelago.

Second only to the dramatic coloration of the sea, the flat, somewhat uniform landscape must be the next feature that draws the visitor's eye. Few large trees are present, with most of the vegetation consisting of cacti and shrubby plants, and one may be forgiven for suspecting that this is not the usual tropical paradise. The 'true' Caribbean islands are, in fact, the granitic Greater and Lesser Antilles that define the border of the Caribbean Sea and were created by volcanic action. Along with excellent soils, many have high mountains that encourage passing cloud formations to deliver their precious cargoes and the land is subsequently able to support lush tropical rainforests that heighten the beauty of these emerald isles. In contrast, the Turks & Caicos, along with the rest of the Bahamas chain, are limestone in origin and all are low-lying, with the highest peak being less than 200 feet above sea level.

Rather than being formed by a violent eruption that thrusts molten rock high above the crashing waves, the Turks & Caicos were produced by a gradual rising of the seabed over millions of years. To understand the processes involved it is best to picture a scene in which the water has been removed to reveal the seascape beneath. Had a fisherman been bobbing about in a boat a few hundred yards north of the islands he would now be

Robust branches of Elkhorn Coral *(Acropora palmata)* jut out from the reef alongside the delicate plates of the similarly coloured Fire Coral *(Millepora complanata)*. The limestone skeletons of these colonial animals make up the vast majority of their bulk, with their living tissues being confined to the outer surfaces and forming a carpet of tiny creatures, each one looking somewhat like an anemone.

During the day, most corals protect their tentacles by retracting them into their skeletons, leaving the algae within their tissues to harness the sun's energy and provide food for the colony. Here, a Great Star Coral *(Montastrea cavernosa)* can be seen with the living animal tightly held against its skeleton. At night it looks very different, with all the polyps extended, each one pushing any captured prey through its own mouth, but sharing its success through an interconnected gut.

resting at the foot of two awe-inspiring mountains. These impressive peaks would be enormous plateaux having precipitous cliffs that in some areas would exceed a height of 7000 feet. The two flattened summits are what make up the shallow waters of this nation, the larger being the Caicos Bank and the smaller to the east, the Turks Bank. By replacing the Atlantic Ocean in this imaginary setting, it is easy to understand that, where undulations on each plateau break the water's surface, the islands and cays of the Turks & Caicos can be found.

But how did these massive, essentially flat-topped structures form? The current theory is that from the late Mesozoic to the late Cenozoic eras (75 – 1 million years ago) sediments accumulated in huge piles of tiny pinhead-sized particles, formed by the deposition of limestone onto smaller grains of sand. As these 'oölites' built up over time, along with shells and other skeletons, they were cemented together with more calcium carbonate that precipitated directly out of the surrounding ocean. Eventually the waters above the growing seamounts became shallow enough for corals to grow and since then the formation of the islands can be attributed largely to the efforts of reef-building organisms.

So what exactly are these marine engineers of the natural world? No doubt, most people are familiar with the brightly coloured anemones that grace rockpools the world over, but it is their colonial relatives, the corals, that are responsible for the huge structures found in tropical waters. Amazing as it may seem, these small invertebrates have managed to build reefs so large that they can be seen from space.

For many of us, the word 'coral' may conjure up an image of pretty rocks that adorn fish tanks and provide cover for the more animated inhabitants. But these familiar marine curios are merely the external skeletons, the colonial animals that formed them having long since passed on. When alive, their soft living tissues form a thin veneer that covers the outer surfaces of the skeleton, penetrating only a fraction of an inch in order to anchor the animal to its hard crystalline structure. In a simple design, each member of the colony, or polyp, sits within a cup-shaped depression in the skeleton and is attached to its neighbours by a thin connective sheet. Each polyp has a single mouth surrounded by a ring of tentacles that are heavily supplied with stinging cells, known as nematocysts. With this impressive miniature arsenal, these tiny flower-like animals prey voraciously on any small unsuspecting creatures that either stumble into their grasp or are washed onto them by the vagaries of local water movements.

Despite being proficient predators, most reef-building corals receive the vast amount of their nutrition from microscopic organisms that actually live within their own tissues. These 'zooxanthellae' have a mutually beneficial, or symbiotic, relationship with their animal hosts, whereby they derive protection from the rigours of a free-living lifestyle and the corals impose a levy on the food they produce from photosynthesis. More important, however, is that the presence of the algae aids in the production of the limestone skeleton, dramatically increasing the formation of calcium carbonate crystals. With millions of single-celled algae occurring within every polyp, the growth form of the animal in some ways mimics that of land plants, spreading out with branches and sheets to provide optimum light levels for their algal tenants. Perhaps this factor, coupled with the productivity and diversity of the organisms found within this marine habitat, has spawned the common analogy of coral reefs as 'rainforests of the sea'.

One of the most amazing features of a tropical reef is the architectural complexity and variety of growth forms presented by the corals. They range from tiny, delicately branched colonies that appear too fragile to survive anywhere other than in an aquarium, to huge boulders the size of a house, which represent centuries of growth achieved by a single colony. Some species create towering pinnacles that project from the reef like an enchanted castle straight out of a fairy-tale book, while

Although corals are renowned for their many hues, for the most part it is the algae within their tissues that provide the visual kaleidoscope. However, there are exceptions, as these brightly coloured flower corals (*Tubastrea* sp.) lack the single-celled plants associated with their reef-building cousins. Their absence means that these corals have a very slow growth rate, but they have no dependence on light and thrive in places like caves, where other corals present little competition.

Often one of the most breath-taking aspects of visiting a reef is the variety of growth forms adopted by the corals, made all the more astounding by the tiny size and simplicity of the polyps that create such masterpieces. Examples include delicate leaf-like blades *(Agaricia sp.)*, huge mounds that resemble brains *(Diploria strigosa)* and pillars that tower over the seascape *(Dendrogyra cylindrus)*.

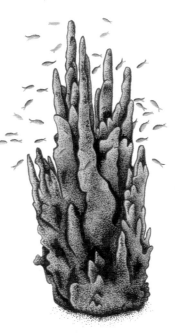

others form hemispherical mounds with meandering surface patterns that give the corals a remarkable brain-like appearance.

In attempting to categorise all this diversity of form, one aspect of coral growth has caused great confusion and frustration for the relentless taxonomists that insist on labelling the natural world: namely that many species adopt strikingly different shapes dependant on their position on the reef. This is mainly a result of varying environmental conditions, such as light levels and wave energy, which change most perceptibly with depth. One species that may be found as a branching colony in the protected shallow waters of the reef-flat can also be found in the deep waters off the slope, forming a low-lying mound with wide plates and lobes, which spread out across the bottom. The deeper a coral lives, the less light it will receive as the sun's rays are absorbed by the seawater; simply by having a larger surface area, more light can be provided to the colony's symbiotic algae. To confuse matters further, stumpy, more compact, or encrusting forms of this species may also be found on the outermost edge of the reef, where the crashing waves dictate the shape most suited to survive their impressive force.

It is not only the individual colonies that have their own growth forms, as the reef itself can take on characteristic shapes. On the windward slopes of the Turks & Caicos reefs it is often possible to see narrow fissures or gullies that are separated by seaward facing buttresses, jutting out at right angles to the incoming waves. This 'spur and groove' formation is created by the power of the oceanic rollers, with their relentless pounding eventually breaking corals and mobilising the accumulated sediments. The disturbed material slides down the reef in much the same way that small rock fragments, or scree, slide down a mountainside, smothering the corals beneath in the process. At the very least, the growth of the affected corals is slowed, whereas colonies on either side of the landslide continue growing normally; over time the difference in growth rates produces gullies and buttresses. In some instances the upper edges of two adjacent 'spurs' can

Dwarfed by the complex, meandering valleys that make up the surface of a Boulder Brain Coral *(Colpophyllia natans)*, a Cleaning Goby *(Gobiosoma genie)* rests upon the thick fleshy tissues. Brain corals have taken the concept of a colony one step further and, instead of daisy-like individuals each sitting in its own skeletal cup, the polyps are merged together in long lines. When extended, tentacles wave from the ridges and a line of mouths punctuates the floor of each valley.

extend so much that they touch, creating a canopy over the gully that ultimately forms a 'swim-through', usually with an opening on the upper reef slope and another lower down on the reef wall. Owing to the lack of light, few coral species grow within these tube-like caverns and with a nice sandy floor created by the gradually sliding sediments, they are popular resting places for some of the larger, more mobile inhabitants of the reef.

With so many corals requiring their own patch to settle and grow, competition for space is rife, with some, such as Elkhorn Coral, becoming specialised to live within certain areas of the reef. Sometimes this species can be found in calm waters where it forms huge, widespread, flattened branches that any rutting deer would be proud to sport. But around the Turks & Caicos, this coral is most readily found within the shallow surge zone of the reef crest, where it receives the brunt of the power from the unremitting waves. Here their chestnut branches grow directly

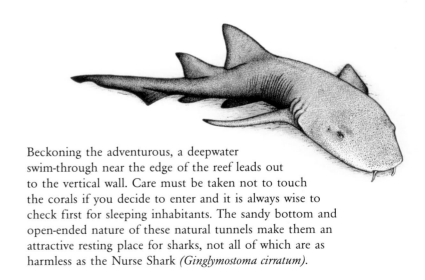

Beckoning the adventurous, a deepwater swim-through near the edge of the reef leads out to the vertical wall. Care must be taken not to touch the corals if you decide to enter and it is always wise to check first for sleeping inhabitants. The sandy bottom and open-ended nature of these natural tunnels make them an attractive resting place for sharks, not all of which are as harmless as the Nurse Shark *(Ginglymostoma cirratum)*.

away from the oncoming surge, the thick, stocky bases acting as a buffer to dissipate the water's energy. So successful is this species at surviving within this region that a dense palisade regularly develops, a living fortification that testifies to the Elkhorn's resilience.

Being able to withstand harsh environmental conditions can always provide a coral with a place to live, but the competition certainly heats up when the reef real estate becomes more desirable. It may be difficult to believe that these seemingly inanimate and slow-growing creatures actually come to blows, but titanic battles between encroaching corals are part of everyday life on the reef. When two corals grow close to one another, the polyps around their borders elongate to form 'sweeper tentacles' that are packed full of stinging cells. Stretching out many times their normal length, these strategic weapons blast holes into their opponent's flanks, in a belligerent effort to retard its advance. Unfortunately for some species, there is a definite hierarchy within these border disputes, with a few heavyweights of the coral world able to push aside all contenders. However, these Goliaths tend to grow more slowly and it is therefore possible for them to be overshadowed by the less powerful species that grow up and over them, out of reach of the blistering punch of their aggressive tentacles.

The competition for space is not only between different coral colonies, as many other organisms require a foothold on the reef, with brightly coloured sponges, sea squirts and hydroids being a few of their invertebrate adversaries. However, the most prevalent rivals fall within a group closely related to coral, that of the gorgonians or sea fans. These animals are also formed by colonies of polyps, but the skeletons they create are soft and flexible. They are commonly seen around the reef as elaborate fans, whips or bushes, gently swaying in the water currents like prairie grasses blown by a summer's breeze. Unlike most hard corals, many of the sea fans extend their polyps during the day, giving their fronds a delicate, fluffy appearance, but one which disguises the fact that they are hunting their waterborne prey.

Waves sweep over the shallow reef crest, where large colonies of Elkhorn Coral *(Acropora palmata)* create a living rampart, their branches growing away from the oncoming rollers. Few species are able to withstand the immense power of the unceasing Atlantic breakers, but this species grows in abundance here, often monopolising this extreme habitat. In doing so, the sturdy colonies dissipate the wave energy and provide a more tolerable environment in their lee.

Corals not only have to compete for space among themselves, but also have to battle against different organisms that find the reef a desirable place to live. A close relative, this Giant Anemone *(Condylactis gigantea)*, which lacks a limestone skeleton, still needs space to secure its soft body and this is usually within a crevice, from which it extends its tentacles to collect food. If threatened by an animal immune to its sting, it can withdraw back into its recess for protection.

Sponges are one of the reef's most common animals, despite showing no obvious signs of animation. While their growth forms vary tremendously, they have a very simple body plan in which the cells are only loosely grouped together. They feed by drawing water in through tiny holes on their surfaces and filtering out food before voiding the water through their large mouth-like openings. Identification is notoriously difficult, but this is probably a Brown Tube Sponge *(Agelas conifera)*.

Once we realise that the hard corals and swaying sea fans belong to the animal kingdom, it may seem that a reef is almost devoid of plant life. It must be remembered, however, that every reef-building coral harbours billions of algal cells and it is the flora that have enabled such a remarkable accumulation of limestone. In addition, the reef's free-living plants are usually small in stature, with larger representatives being closely cropped by the insatiable appetite of the herbivore hordes. Of these 'macroalgae', many species directly contribute to the inorganic bulk of the reef by producing calcareous skeletons of their own, similar to those created by the corals. As they die, their remains add to the white sandy sediments of the reef that not only form the beautiful beaches associated with the Turks & Caicos, but also act like mortar, binding together the building blocks laid down by the corals.

Looking like bleached corals, these White Encrusting Zoanthids *(Palythoa caribaeorum)* belong to their own animal group. They lack a hard skeleton and rely on their stinging tentacles to capture prey, as they have no food-producing algae in their tissues. Many other plants occur on the reef. Here the leathery blades of *Turbinaria* can be seen next to the scroll-like *Padina* and some even have limestone skeletons, like the segmented *Halimeda*.

Reef Relations

The force of the crashing waves may ultimately create the brilliant white sands of the Turks & Caicos by breaking up the coral and algal skeletons, but many other marine organisms offer a helping hand. The relatively soft limestone rock is perfect for animals that seek refuge by digging their own burrows and a protected home can be of paramount importance with the countless mouths that patrol the reef. Even while coral tissues are still forming their calcium carbonate support, any exposed areas of the skeleton, such as the base, are open to attack from these 'bioeroding' marauders. In their efforts to secure a safe retreat they often excavate the very foundations of their homes, eventually causing the structure to crumble and the coral to succumb to the action of the waves. Soft-bodied worms are one of the main culprits of this natural vandalism, but sponges, bivalve molluscs and other animals are also involved. Some attack the living areas of the coral, tunnelling into the skeleton on the upper surfaces and then maintaining their entrance hole by preventing repair attempts by their host. Eventually the colony and burrow grow in synchrony, the polyps occasionally creating a raised lip around the portal of their uninvited guest. The Christmas Tree Worm is one of the reef's most noticeable excavators, its brightly coloured appendages sometimes littering the surfaces of boulder-shaped colonies like fairy lights. Each worm has a pair of fir-tree-shaped gills that extend outside its shelter and are modified for feeding. Rapid changes in local light levels, or water movements, which may suggest the approach of an intruder, elicit a lightning response from the worm, its gills being quickly retracted into its burrow and the entrance plugged by a protective cone.

In addition to invertebrates undermining the activities of the reef builders, an abundance of parrotfish in the Turks & Caicos considerably augments the conversion of coral into sediments. These large, often gaudy fish have modified jaws that form beak-like crushing plates, which are used to scrape the rock. While some species simply graze the surface, others have the capacity to remove sizeable chunks. Whether they actually intend to dine on the living coral tissues is uncertain, but in general their feeding is directed towards the turf algae

Predator-prey relationships on a reef are not always as obvious as sharks eating smaller fish. This beautifully patterned Flamingo Tongue *(Cyphoma gibbosum)* is actually eating the bright purple sea fan on which it rests. Seemingly innocent associations can represent life or death struggles, though the presence of a Christmas Tree Worm *(Spirobranchus giganteus)* has little effect on its coral host.

Stopping to take a bite of algae-covered rock, a Princess Parrotfish *(Scarus taeniopterus)* is one of the reef's many excavators. Parrotfish have a rather complex and intriguing sex life, passing through three phases as they mature, often marked by a dramatic change in shape, colour and markings. The intermediate phase includes both males and females, whereas the terminal phase, pictured above, is always a mature male, often being the result of a female undergoing a sex change.

that grow like miniature lawns across unoccupied areas of the reef. But since these diminutive plants often penetrate the porous limestone, greater quantities of food can be harvested by biting into the rock and grinding the rubble. After digesting what they can, the fish void the sediments, often trailing behind them a white chalky curtain as they swim over the reef with nonchalant flicks of their pectoral fins.

While the parrotfish excavate their preferred nourishment, one fish family has developed a special relationship with the ubiquitous turf algae, which, if left unpruned, would form a fine emerald sheet over much of the reef. Damselfish are the reef's gardeners, each individual standing guard over its own private algal patch. Like an irate farmer chasing trespassers away, these pugnacious little fish take on all comers in defence of their valuable crop. Less desirable plants are weeded out with well-aimed bites, with yesterday's meal becoming a natural fertiliser for tomorrow's fodder in this mutually beneficial arrangement.

Another reef vegetarian is the Long-Spined Sea Urchin that also spends its life munching the ever-present algae. But unlike the damselfish, their diet is less discerning, with the urchins eating virtually every scrap of plant life they come across. So effective are they in their foraging, they often form halos of white sand around isolated coral outcrops, where they have completely denuded the surrounding area of its floral cover. Their numbers, however, are still recovering from a natural virus that decimated the species across the whole of its range during the early 1980s. Although the Turks & Caicos were little affected, many Caribbean reefs were subsequently overgrown by algae, a testament to the pruning capabilities of these spiky animals. This event also demonstrated that seemingly insignificant creatures can play a pivotal role in the natural balance of this precious marine ecosystem. Although it may appear that the exceedingly long spines of these urchins would make them a conspicuous member of the reef community, they are rarely seen, spending their days hidden in crevices and beneath overhangs. As with

many of the reef's scavengers, they wait for the night's dark shroud before venturing out, improving their chances of survival as the visually dependant predators rest from their daytime prowls. Though they move more freely after dusk, danger still lurks in the form of some opportunistic hunters that have adopted nocturnal pursuits. During the day, French Grunts huddle together with Mahogany Snappers beneath the branches of an Elkhorn Coral, but with the setting sun the schools dissipate and these predators join the other animals working the night shift.

In an effort to avoid becoming a meal, many reef creatures adopt camouflage as a ploy, but in the hands of the hunter this form of concealment becomes a double-edged sword, allowing an ambush or stealthy approach to go unobserved. Many of the reef animals have chameleon-like qualities, being able to change their colours and body patterning like theatrical costumes. But the prize must surely belong to the octopus, whose kaleidoscopic skin is covered with pigment cells that have an unrivalled ability to mimic their surroundings with stunning speed and accuracy. Being nocturnal hunters, they use their capacity for camouflage

Trumpetfish *(Aulostomus maculatus)* often change their colour and use their odd shape to blend in with their surroundings. Here one hangs head down among the branches of a rope sponge, avoiding the attention of predators and waiting to snap up its next meal. The bizarre patterns of a Honeycomb Cowfish *(Lactophrys polygonia)* help to break-up its outline when hiding, but it too has the ability to change colour before your eyes.

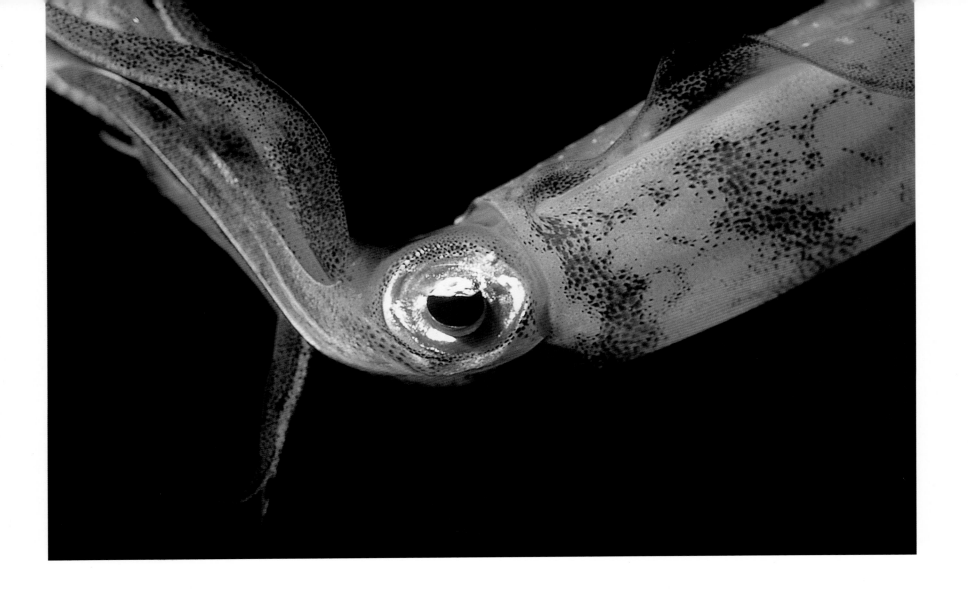

The large, iridescent eye of a Caribbean Reef Squid *(Sepioteuthis sepioidea)* stares with curiosity into the lens of the camera, leaving you in no doubt as to the intelligence of these highly complex invertebrates. Their eight arms are often held in this odd, almost prayer-like position, while the two elastic tentacles used to catch their prey are rarely seen, kept hidden within their crown of arms.

as a form of self-preservation, allowing them to spend the daylight hours safe in their anonymity. At night they pillage the reef, detecting their quarry by chemicals in the water and feeding on any tasty morsels their suckered arms can secure.

A close relative of the octopus is the Caribbean Reef Squid, which also hunts by night using long, extendable tentacles to grasp unsuspecting prey. During the day they hover above the reef in small schools, their translucent bodies shimmering with rainbows of colour, like some ethereal alien of science fiction. As if trying to communicate with an approaching swimmer, they flash bursts of colour in complex patterns across their bodies, constantly watching with their oversized eyes, perhaps waiting for an intelligent response. Manoeuvring themselves with slight changes of their undulating fins, they maintain an acceptable distance, but any transgressions are met with a magician's puff of smoke as they leave behind a cloud of ink to conceal their jet-propelled retreat.

With so many animals feeding on one another, there is a definite hierarchy among the hunters, with size playing the predominant role. Near the top of the food chain, the larger individuals of the rapacious throng comprise some of the more charismatic species that grace the waters of the Turks & Caicos. A common sight is the Great Barracuda, its silvery scales shining in the sunlight like a new suit of armour. Decked out for battle with a fearsome array of dagger-shaped teeth, this fish usually hangs motionless in the water column, its large saucer-like eyes watching the day-to-day routine of the reef with an aloof yet curious air. However, its placid demeanour is nothing to become complacent about. Although this intimidating species poses no danger to humans, the perspective is very different if you happen to be a small fish that has strayed just that bit too far from cover. The barracuda's long cigar-shaped body consists mainly of potent muscle blocks that, with a flick of its tail, transform this seemingly relaxed bystander into a lunging beast. Bearing down like a live torpedo shot from an undetected submarine, its

Great Barracuda *(Sphyraena barracuda)*, like sharks, have suffered from sensational stories that have exaggerated their infamy, though these are based on their menacing appearance rather than any reports of unprovoked attacks. To the recreational diver these fish may look dangerous, but in fact they pose no threat, apart from the shock of finding a four foot predator hovering behind you, as they are inquisitive creatures and often follow divers around the reef.

careless prey stands little chance, with those menacing teeth designed to lock onto small slippery bodies with no hint of reprieve.

Many other large, silvery predators of the Turks & Caicos belong to the jack family, with some species, such as the Horse-Eye Jack, tending to congregate during the daytime in impressive, slowly circling schools. With safety in numbers, these gatherings sometimes constitute hundreds of individuals that form a spiralling wall of eyes, which both scan for danger and look out for the shimmering clouds of Silversides upon which they feed. The bountiful reef also occasionally attracts more pelagic visitors from the adjacent deep water, such as the African Pompano. This outrageously lustrous fish tends to be more solitary in nature, its presence usually being revealed by sudden flashes of light along the reef edge that are produced by its mirror-like scales reflecting the sun's rays.

The boldly striped Nassau Grouper is another familiar predator of the local reefs and typifies the prevalent fish family to which it belongs. Slowly patrolling its home territory and always staying close to the corals, it hunts smaller fish and invertebrates, again, like the barracuda, exuding a casual demeanour until it is time to strike. Rapidly covering short distances, the final blow of its surprise attack is the powerful suction created upon opening its large cavernous mouth, which helps to draw in any fleeing critters. The edge of the jaw may only be rimmed with small needle-like teeth, but inside its maw these sharp projections are found in their thousands, covering the tongue and palate and allowing the grouper to grasp its prey before swallowing it whole.

The reef may seem like an endless 'fish-eat-fish' world, but the Nassau Grouper, along with many other marine species, is a regular participant in a non-combatant relationship with smaller individuals, where the usual predator-prey conflict is suspended for a mutually agreeable pastime. The grouper approaches a designated area, usually marked by a prominent coral outcrop,

Nassau Groupers *(Epinephelus striatus)* can adopt many different hues, from very pale to almost entirely black, and this can result in their banding pattern being sometimes difficult to discern. These colour changes may be brought about by the fish's mood, or by its environment to aid camouflage, but whatever its shade, this species can always be identified by the black saddle mark at the base of its tail.

and floats head down or rests on the bottom in a torpid state, its gills flared out and its huge mouth agape. This posture is a sign to the reef's domestic workers that their skills are sought after and the grouper is soon joined by several tiny gobies and shrimps that inhabit this 'cleaning station'. Like industrious little elves, they set about the task of meticulously cleansing the skin of their over-sized companion, feeding on bothersome parasites and removing dead flecks of tissue. The more adventurous among them will even enter the mouth, grooming the gills and flossing the teeth of their would-be assassin. When satiated, the grouper gives a distinctive shudder and its entourage retreats to its coral promontory, before the predator resumes its place in the hierarchy.

No reference to life and death on a reef would be complete without mentioning the pinnacle of the food chain, a position most suitably occupied by the requiem sharks. A common representative in the Turks & Caicos is the Reef Shark, which can

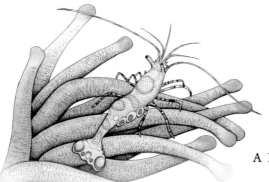

A Porcupinefish *(Diodon hystrix)* looks as if it is enjoying the attentions of a tiny Cleaning Goby *(Gobiosoma genie)* that is carefully grooming the skin between its spines. But fish are not the only ones to cash in on the predatory armistice afforded by offering a valeting service. Crustaceans, like the Spotted Cleaner Shrimp *(Periclimenes yucatanicus)*, are also involved, waving their antennae in an effort to attract new customers.

Dolphins have long been held as the epitome of grace and
freedom, a view that no doubt stems from their sleek
bodies and what seems to be an unrelenting display of
playful exuberance. Appearing in the mythology of many
cultures, they have been revered as gods, as well as
messengers from distant planets, and their leaping forms are
a common sight in the waters around the Turks & Caicos.

regularly be seen cruising the drop-off either alone or in pairs. Unlike the slow approach practised by the groupers, these predators move swiftly over the coral, making rapid directional changes in an elegant ballet that belies their intent. They have suffered a great deal of bad press over the years, but most people catch only a fleeting glimpse before the fish disappear into the blue.

Among the many deep-water visitors to local reefs, a pod of Bottlenose or Atlantic Spotted Dolphins must surely evoke some

of the greatest feelings of wonderment in the chance observer. The beauty and grace with which they cavort within their aquatic realm are matched only by the control they exert over their obvious power. To be swimming off a beach and then see one of these air-breathing mammals effortlessly rocket towards you, only to veer off at the last second with a playful squeak, clearly demonstrates our limitations in this alien environment. While the pulsing clicks and shrill whistles may seem like idle chatter, this perceptive animal is in fact using the sounds to assess its surroundings and communicate with its family group. Behind

Despite the amazing lengths to which flatfish have evolved to camouflage and conceal themselves, they are no real match for a hungry Bottlenose Dolphin *(Tursiops truncatus)*. The wary Peacock Flounder *(Bothus lunatus)* always stays close to the sandy bottom and will often bury itself, leaving only its eyes exposed and alert for danger. But all this visual deception becomes irrelevant when one of your hunters is equipped with sonar.

the jovial smile are the teeth of a predator and the high, intelligent looking forehead is this hunter's secret weapon. Although dolphins have large brains, their bulbous 'melon' is not caused by cerebral development; rather it harbours fatty, oil-filled tissues that are used to focus the sound clicks made at the base of the blowhole. Like bats, dolphins have the ability to echolocate, painting their world with sound in order to find, among other things, their prey. By beaming a stream of high pitched pulses over a sandy patch and interpreting the returning echoes, a dolphin can determine the exact location of a hidden meal, seeking refuge beneath the concealing sediments. A few prods from a judiciously placed beak can elicit a last-ditch swim for cover from an exposed flounder. Should the dolphin's lightning reflexes fail to snap it up, it is thought that this remarkable creature can render its prey helpless by stunning them with a concentrated burst of sound, thereby delivering an acoustic 'coup de grâce'.

The Flowering Pioneers

Plants are the driving force behind virtually every natural system on the planet. By harnessing the sun's energy, they are able to create tissues from simple compounds such as water and carbon dioxide, a process that releases oxygen into the atmosphere and subsequently succours the demands of the world's aerobic animals. In the case of a coral reef, different species of algae also assist the reef building corals with the formation of their skeletons, as well as producing and cementing much of the sediments. But there are two types of flowering plants that have been integral to the development of the Turks & Caicos Islands and remain essential to their future geological stability. These are the seagrasses and mangroves that grace the coastal waters, where they give rise to their own unique habitats and act as a final buffer to the erosive power of the incoming waves.

There are two main species of seagrass that occur around the islands, Turtle Grass and Manatee Grass. Growing together or alone, these plants form dense aquatic lawns that cover the sand flats, creating mosaics of dark shapes within the shallow turquoise waters. Turtle Grass, with its flat ribbon-like foliage, is by far the most common species and its presence in the adjacent waters is made obvious since detached leaves generally sink to the bottom and wash up in piles along the strandline. Manatee Grass, on the other hand, is more spaghetti-like and pieces tend to float on the surface after breaking away, forming buoyant mats that can drift far out to sea. Like their land-based contemporaries, seagrasses grow from their base, which might suggest that they too receive incessant cropping from herbivores. But, with the notable exceptions of Green Turtles, Manatees and Long-Spined Sea Urchins, few animals feed upon the tough green blades and therefore, the overall grazing pressure seagrasses receive is surprisingly low. However, occupying the sandy expanses of the well-lit shallows has its drawbacks, as the leaf surfaces offer pole position for other plants that are unable to maintain a foothold in the shifting sediments. With no root system to speak of, many species of algae survive within this habitat as 'epiphytes', attaching themselves to the stable sea-grasses instead of to the sand. What is more, the

A young Green Sea Turtle *(Chelonia mydas)* leisurely swims in search of the most succulent seagrass stems, evidently spoilt for choice amongst the thick beds adjacent to White House Reef, Providenciales. Despite the abundance of these marine flowering plants, few animals are able to feed on their leaves and most, like seahorses, simply seek refuge within their foliage.

seagrass fronds attract many animals, such as sponges and bryozoans, which usually encrust over a more stable substratum. With all this extraneous growth, the leaves eventually become weighed down and the green photosynthetic pigments within them overshadowed by their prolific covering. But these marine plants have evolved a unique adaptation to this problem; their long, slender shoots have several structural weak points that cause them to snap when placed under undue strain. Hence, the arrival of a tropical storm agitates the shallows and causes any leaves over-encumbered with an excess of attached organisms to break, so freeing the younger sections closer to the sand from the burden of their uninvited guests.

Seagrasses are in fact the only flowering plants that have adapted to a fully submerged marine lifestyle. Apart from their amazing ability to cope with saltwater, they produce waterborne pollen to fertilise their tiny submerged flowers and their leaves have air pockets to aid in support. They also have highly developed root systems with underground stems that spread out laterally below

Many species of algae stand like miniature trees scattered among the tufts of seagrass. With no true roots, the algae are attached to buried pieces of rubble by their holdfasts. If the sands were to shift they would be likely to topple over, but the extensive root system of the seagrasses helps by stabilising the sediments. In addition, the gently swaying ribbon-like fronds offer shelter for numerous animals, including the ever-present Bluehead (*Thalassoma bifasciatum*).

the sand, extending roots downwards from nodes dispersed along their lengths. In addition to providing support, these 'rhizomes' give rise to new plants that push up through the sand and extend the reign of their cloning parent, much like the runners in a strawberry patch. Beneath a seagrass bed, the rhizomes and roots of each plant become interwoven in a matrix of vegetable matter that far outweighs what can be seen from above. This intricate web serves to bind the loose sediments together, forming a stable foundation that can be several feet thick. Sometimes, at the edges of their influence, where the sand has been washed away by water movements, small banks form that reveal the extent of the root network and provide an insight into the importance of these submerged meadows to the nearby coral reefs. The absence of such a 'coastal door-mat' would lead to far greater mobility of those beautiful white sands and the corals would subsequently have to cope with much greater sediment loads.

Besides their ability to consolidate the sands, the presence of seagrasses also improves water clarity, as their gently swaying leaves have the effect of slowing the prevailing currents and causing the water to lose a large proportion of its suspended matter. With their extensive roots stabilising the shifting seabed and their blades above providing cover while taming the movements of the shallow waters, it is not surprising that seagrass meadows represent an important refuge for the sea's smaller creatures. Along with the resident animal life, many other species spend their early years within the relative safety of these protected grounds, either feeding on the abundant algae or capturing prey smaller than themselves. But, given this high concentration of 'easy' food items, it is little wonder that the more intrepid predators are attracted off the reef. Juvenile Lemon Sharks make regular sorties into the shallows as the tide rises to give access to the more near-shore areas. Spotted Eagle Rays fly in well co-ordinated squadrons over the beds in search of suitable areas to rummage the sand for molluscs, while a solitary Southern Stingray lies half submerged in the sand, using its concealed mouth to make light work of any buried inhabitants.

Slowly cruising between the pneumatophore roots and submerged lower branches of a mangrove stand, a juvenile Lemon Shark *(Negaprion brevirostris)* takes advantage of an exceptionally high tide to snap up any unwary individuals. The sheltered areas created by the root systems of these salt-tolerant trees are important nursery grounds for many marine species, with the wooden latticework still offering sanctuary despite the presence of this top predator.

Because of this influx of larger predators during high tide, many of the more mobile species retreat with the rising waters, while others either rely on their camouflage, or conceal themselves below the surface of the sand. Those that routinely evacuate this seagrass 'bistro' usually find sanctuary within the submerged

Like a vampire flying from its crypt, a Southern Stingray *(Dasyatis americana)* launches from its resting-place, cloaked in billowing clouds of white sand. The pectoral fins of these fish are greatly enlarged, allowing them to flap their 'wings' in a form of underwater flight. Having a mouth on their underside, they create circular depressions in the sand by pushing their bodies down, often becoming buried up to their eyes in their search for food.

roots of the other flowering pioneers that push forward the frontiers of the land – the mangroves. These trees are not as fully marine as their seagrass cousins, but have considerable adaptations for life on the edge. Since trees elevate their branches high into the air, there is a greater potential for strong winds to blow them over and so their root systems are usually set deep below the ground to afford them adequate support. However, roots require oxygen to survive and, in the case of mangroves, this cannot be found within the soil, which is poorly aerated due to the permeating seawater. Therefore, their roots only extend a few feet into the sand and their structure has been modified to supply their subterranean extremities with more oxygen, while still providing the trees sufficient support.

The Turks & Caicos are home to three true mangrove species, two of which are very similar in appearance, namely the Black and White Mangroves. Other than being a little stunted, at first glance these species look like quite normal trees, especially at high tide when the sea laps around their gnarled trunks. But as the water recedes, the adaptations of their root systems become apparent, with each tree surrounded by what appears to be an over-sized bed of nails. Long, thick 'cable roots' radiate out from beneath an individual tree, extending well beyond the reach of their elevated branches, though lying just below the surface of the sediments. Like guy ropes for a marquee, these roots provide the tree with much needed support, but they too need to be supplied with oxygen, which is the job of the 'pneumatophores'. Appearing as thin, blunt spikes that sprout up along the length of the submerged cable roots, these special structures are covered with tiny openings that take up air, acting as ventilation shafts and preventing their parent tissues from suffocating within the anoxic sands. For many creatures of the sea, these finger-like projections provide the first line of defence against the tidal movement of predators.

The true botanical ramparts, however, are constructed by the roots of one other species, the Red Mangrove, the immersed

Prop roots of the Red Mangrove *(Rhizophora mangle)* extend out to sea in an effort to anchor the parent plants. Thinner aerial roots can also be seen arching away from the upper branches and joining the confusion of struts embedded into the sand. Although both types of roots barely penetrate the muddy surface, they not only carry out the function of support, but also take up nutrients and supply their underground portions with the oxygen they need to survive.

portions of which constitute an important cage-like nursery habitat. Instead of trying to create support by growing long extensions beneath the ground's unwelcome environment, the trunk of this tree produces downward curving branches that form short rootlets where they contact the sand. Like the hand of a pool player forming a bridge for the cue, these 'prop roots' provide a sturdy support, without the need to anchor the tree far below the surface. As the true branches stretch out from the main trunk, they produce thin aerial roots that grow down to the sediments and then consolidate their vertical form by expanding their girth. The resulting struts eventually become like new tree trunks, helping to make the area beneath a Red Mangrove canopy a confusion of tangled, looping wood, especially where the roots of neighbouring trees interweave.

Within the coastal forests of the Turks & Caicos it is the Red Mangrove that is the true pioneer, always on the outermost edges, extending its prop roots seawards like wooden hands grasping new territories. But it is the seedlings that have the most astounding adaptations for colonising new lands. Requiring no dormant stage, the seeds will germinate while still attached to the adult plant and grow to around a foot in length. The main emphasis of this early development is the production of a long, heavy stake-like structure called the 'hypocotyl' that hangs down towards the ground. If the tide is out when it eventually breaks away, the fall from the branches causes the hypocotyl to penetrate the sediments and a rapid deployment of rootlets can secure a place beside its parent. On the other hand, a seedling may plunge into the encroaching waters, where it floats like a raft

Two Nurse Sharks *(Ginglymostoma cirratum)* have chosen what seems to be a rather uncomfortable place to rest among the pneumatophores of a nearby mangrove. These bottom-living sharks are nocturnal hunters, using the sensory barbels either side of their small mouths to help detect prey hidden within the sediments. Although generally considered harmless, they have been known to bite if provoked.

destined to leave its parental home. With a remarkable tolerance to salty conditions, the young plant can now set sail for distant lands, drifting with the water currents in a passive voyage of discovery. If it is eventually washed ashore like some shipwrecked mariner, the right conditions can allow it to set about forming a new colony, firmly planting the mangrove flag on the beaches of its newfound terrain.

Although the local mangrove species never grow very tall, they can form small, isolated forests that not only create an aquatic nursery with their root systems, but also provide a home for the animals that are able to reach their branches and adapt to an arboreal existence. As with any trees, numerous insects inhabit their bounds, whether flying around the foliage or burrowed into the bark, and, in turn, these are preyed upon by a few opportunistic reptilian species. But by far the most splendid

Seedlings or propagules of the Red Mangrove develop while still attached to the tree, their unusual, long green bodies eventually breaking away from the brown, nut-like fruits. The flowers, on the other hand, are quite inconspicuous, with the hairy, white petals lasting only a few hours. They leave behind the yellow-green casings that protected the buds, which can still be seen as curls at the base of each fruit.

visitors that seek refuge amongst the mangrove leaves must be the birds. Here they feed on the plentiful supply of buzzing invertebrates, or use the added height to sit and wait for an unsuspecting seafood meal.

One of the most impressive visitors is the Magnificent Frigatebird, which forms large nesting colonies often precariously perched on the uppermost limits of a tree. During the breeding season, hundreds of individuals can be found at the tiny mangrove-covered cay known as Man O' War Bush, just off the southern coast of Middle Caicos. Some may be engaged in noisy squabbles with their neighbours, but most fly high above the island in a hovering black swarm. Each bird resembles a child's kite held to the small forest below by an invisible string, able to hang motionless by facing into a headwind and harnessing the slightest air movements with its long, narrow outstretched wings. From their elevated position the birds can keep a wary eye open for any threats to their gawky looking chicks that may approach from the sea or from along the swath of brilliant white sand that is the shoreline extending beyond their mangrove outpost.

As if waiting for applause, a Yellow Warbler *(Dendroica petechia)* takes a well-earned rest from performing its melodic song. This vocal and brightly coloured bird likes to deliver its recitals from the dense cover provided by mangroves, a habit that has earned it the alternative name of the Mangrove Canary. The males can be distinguished from the females by the chestnut streaks that stripe their yellow breasts.

Chicks of the Magnificent Frigatebird *(Fregata magnificens)* sit perched on top of a mangrove stand, fully feathered and well able to fly. Despite this, their black-headed mothers care for them for up to five months after fledging, when they are at last able to fend for themselves. The all black males are less devoted and are often seen with their red throat patches inflated in a flamboyant courtship display.

Littorally Living

The tidal habitat that forms the interface between the land and sea is known as the littoral zone. The organisms that live within this coastal region have had to adapt to a twice-daily immersion in saltwater, coupled with the exposure to the air that results from the tide's vacillations. Even the land plants that occur high up the beach, beyond the range of the greatest spring tides, have to cope with the constant sea spray that can block their fine pores and result in brown scorch marks on their otherwise green foliage. Marine animals, abandoned by the retreating waters, must either absorb oxygen from the air or trap enough water close to their gills to sustain respiratory demands until the return of their fluid environment. Their problems are made worse by the damaging potential of the baking sun, which can desiccate not only their soft tissues, but also evaporate their precious water supply, suffocating any affected individuals. A further predicament posed by this transitory habitat is the alternation between two sets of predators. At low tide, the land-based hunters steal into previously inaccessible areas, snatching up the unwary sea creatures, while at high tide their marine counterparts move in for the kill. However, the most influential factor experienced within this zone must be the water motion itself. Often whipped up by distant winds, the waves that roll in with the tides smash against the shore, scouring and literally sandblasting the resident life. Although somewhat dissipated by the fringing reefs, it is these forces that have shaped the coastlines and accumulated the sands into wondrous beaches.

As if in the hands of an artist, the rocky shores are moulded and sculpted by the sea and the creatures that live within this dynamic environment must cling to their existence with a tenacious grip. Undoubtedly, the masters of this niche are the shelled molluscs, which use their muscular pad, or 'foot', to secure them to the rocks. During low tide, large congregations of snail-like Nerites can be found taking refuge in the hollows carved out by the wave action. Another common resident of the Turks & Caicos is the Fuzzy Chiton, a primitive relative of the more familiar limpet. These strange lozenge-shaped animals are characterised by eight armoured plates that protect their vulnerable bodies in an arrangement somewhat resembling the bands of an armadillo. Perhaps as an adaptation

The Atlantic Ocean gently laps against the leeward shore of North West Point, Providenciales, where rocky outcrops punctuate the white sandy beaches. Whether the sea flows over rock or sand, the area lying within the tidal range is known as the 'littoral zone'. Due to its variable nature and vulnerability to storms, this is a very harsh environment, but one in which many organisms have adapted to live.

It may be difficult to believe that the high craggy cliffs seen on some of the islands were formed by marine creatures, but a closer inspection of the rocks will often reveal the presence of marine fossils. Here, a cross-section of a coral skeleton can be seen embedded in a weathered piece of ancient reef found on the northern shore of Middle Caicos. With evidence like this, it is easier to accept the notion that the Turks & Caicos were once submerged.

to avoid being dislodged, they move at an incredibly slow rate, grazing on the turf algae that coats the sea-drenched rocks.

While watching the breakers march in from the Atlantic Ocean and crash into the cliffs on the windward edge of the Turks & Caicos, it may be perplexing to consider the origin of the land. If the islands were formed by the activities of marine organisms, how can they have created rocky structures that rise, in some areas, fifty feet out of the sea? The answer is that over geological time the level of the oceans has fluctuated as a response to the amount of water held within the polar ice caps. During warmer eras, more pack ice melted than froze and the sea level rose accordingly. As this increase was so gradual, occurring over a vast time scale, the growth of the coral reef organisms was able to keep in step with the slow rate of submergence. However, in colder times when the global temperature dropped and the world was plunged into an ice age, the areas that were once covered by the sea were left high and dry as the water became locked into the advancing glaciers. When viewed from a human perspective, it can be difficult to appreciate the time scales involved in these processes, but something that may seem so permanent a feature, like the amount of water in the sea, can be a highly variable factor when measured against a few billion years of Earth history. As a result of these fluctuations, ancient reefs that were once teeming with marine life now form the craggy cliffs and raised limestone headlands of this island nation.

In addition to the weathered surfaces of these exposed reefs, the local waters wash over another form of rock that has purely inorganic origins. 'Beachrock' is often revealed at low tide and is formed below the surface of the sand by the precipitation of calcium carbonate. This process is not governed by either flora or fauna as the limestone is simply produced by the percolation of both seawater and rainwater through the sediments. Complete hardening only occurs after tidal erosion has washed away the overlying sand and the atmosphere has had a chance to work on this newly revealed sedimentary rock.

The presence of this beachrock is an unwelcome obstacle for one marine animal that has to return to the land in order to reproduce. Sea turtles are perfectly adapted to their aquatic lifestyle, but the flippers that afford them such grace in the oceans are barely adequate to haul their bulky shell-encased bodies up a sandy incline. Once a suitable area has been reached, the turtle proceeds to dig a deep hole in which she lays around a hundred leathery eggs. Upon finishing, she packs the sand back onto the egg chamber and, with the completion of her maternal duties, lumbers down the beach to the freedom of the sea. After a couple of months, the offspring emerge from their sand-covered nest and the baby turtles scamper towards the water. During this stage of their life natural predation is high, as they represent bite-sized treats for many land and marine predators. For this reason they swim straight off the reef and begin an epic journey to the Sargasso Sea, over 1000 miles west of Florida, where they stay for many years feeding mainly on jellyfish. Whether a hatchling will ever traverse another beach depends upon the temperature of the surrounding sand during incubation, as surprisingly this factor determines their sex. The males will never venture on land again, though the females are destined to return to the very same beach in more than twenty years time, when they will clamber up the sand to lay eggs of their own.

Miniature cliffs formed by eroded beachrock are washed by the rising tide, the water foaming between the boulders it helped to create. Coastlines fringed by this sedimentary rock are unsuitable for nesting turtles, which require areas of soft sand. The hatchlings that are produced emerge into a world with many dangers and one that is increasingly hostile for these ancient reptiles.

Usually Green Turtles *(Chelonia mydas)* use the cover of darkness to clamber up the beach and lay their soft leathery eggs in a sandy nest. However, this lone female has been caught out by the increasing light of dawn as it lumbers towards the sea, the flippers that provide it with such agility below the waves being ill-equipped to manage anything more than an ungainly crawl across this alien terrain.

As on the rocky shore, there are associated hardships with eking out a livelihood within the shifting beach sands, but this unstable habitat has many advantages too. The large particle size of the coarse-grained sand, coupled with the highly oxygenated surf, ensures that these sediments are well aerated and the ceaseless tides also bring with them a plentiful supply of food. Abundant filter feeders hide within the sand, feasting on the particles of organic debris and plankton they can strain from the waters that bathe them. Once again, it is the molluscs that dominate this habitat, their often double-valved shells protecting their filters from the scouring action of the moving sand. The abounding presence of these covert creatures is usually only revealed upon their death, when the waves scatter their beautifully painted and intricately sculptured dwellings amongst the biological refuse that forms the strandline.

This darkened line of encrusted seagrass fronds and assorted flotsam is the focus for many of the more mobile beach residents. With the dwindling waters, an army of crustaceans emerges. They appear in a flurry of sand as they excavate their burrows, or like an apparition, slowly solidifying above the surface, their ghost-like entrance provided by deft movements of their multiple appendages. If the coast is clear, they scuttle over to the strandline to inspect the most recent delivery of dead and dying matter that has been washed ashore. Hermit crabs rummage through the natural litter, perhaps in search of a new mobile home. Shells long since vacated by the original occupants afford these soft-bodied crabs with good protection, but their continued growth requires that their adopted abodes be regularly exchanged for larger ones. Some crab species appear disinterested by the strandline, preferring to work over the sand immediately adjacent to their burrows, forming intricate radial patterns that are destroyed by the arrival of the next tide. Others seem more intent on display, like the tiny but animated Fiddler Crabs. Each male waves his oversized redundant claw like a violinist playing an unheard symphony, a performance presumably appreciated by its female counterpart.

Along with deserted mollusc shells, the strandline also holds many remains of lesser-known animals. The translucent quill of a squid, used as a support for its soft body; the floats of small jellyfish, blown to the land by unfavourable winds; sponges ripped free from their seabed moorings; and the hardened tunics of sea squirts are but a few examples of the fascinating curios yielded by the sea. Sometimes the bleached skeletons of heart urchins and sand dollars can be found, their delicate structures usually being crushed by the action of the waves. When alive, these animals roam like moles beneath the sand, their mane of tube feet and spines allowing them to tunnel through the sediments. Rather than filtering the water, they engulf the sand itself, digesting the organic content and voiding the remains as their burrows close behind them. A close relative, the starfish, can often be found combing the shallow waters of the beach, their internal hydraulic system extending and contracting tube feet on their underside, so that they gradually glide over the sands with imperceptible effort. For all their lack of animation, starfish are surprisingly one of the many marine predators that often hunt the sandy slopes at high tide. But perhaps the most successful hunters of this changeable habitat are the birds, their specialised bills, keen senses and wondrous variety being so well exhibited in the Turks & Caicos.

Far from being barren deserts, the wide expanses of sand that make up the many beaches contain within them a multitude of buried organisms. Most numerous are the bivalves, like the Sunrise Tellin *(Tellina radiata)*, which each have two hinged shells to protect their soft bodies from the shifting grains of sand. Safe within their home-grown refuge, they suck in and filter the seawater, feeding on the organic particles they find.

An intricate network of armour plates and short spines covers the body of the Cushion Sea Star *(Oreaster reticulatus)*. Often found scattered over the sandy shallows, these creatures are invariably feeding with their stomachs held outside their bodies to digest any organic matter. They are also able to prey on clams, sliding their stomachs between the closed shells to liquefy the animal within its home.

Working through the natural debris of the strandline, a Ghost Crab *(Ocypode quadrata)* pauses from its toil, as if to watch the last few minutes of the setting sun. These swift crustaceans have gained their spiritual reputation by the disappearing act they perform, achieved by making a short dash then flattening their bodies to the ground, eliminating any shadows and using their colour to blend into the sand.

CHAPTER TWO

The Land above the Waves

Flights of Fancy

In the dimming light of a spent sunset, a small plover scampers along the water's edge as the sea washes over a sandy shore. Running up and down the beach with the ebb and flow of each wave, the bird appears to be suffering from the indecision of a reluctant bather, wanting to go for a swim but unwilling to take that first plunge. Despite the plover's haste, the scene is one of tranquillity, heightened by the remnants of the day's warmth and the soft lapping of the breaking waves. But all this activity from the feathered performer is neither recreational frivolity, nor the prelude to a quick dip before bedtime. The bird is working for its supper, an efficient predator hunting the sand in the wake of each receding wave for the slightest sign of its invertebrate prey.

With so many molluscs, crustaceans and worms inhabiting the sand, it is little wonder that a whole suite of birds is keen to take advantage of this plentiful food supply. Flocks of Ruddy Turnstones are regularly seen in the Turks & Caicos, rummaging through the strandline, the intricate patterns of their plumage affording a surprising degree of camouflage against the rocky shores. Using their short, slightly up-turned bills, they scour the beaches, literally overturning stones to reveal the marine creatures that seek refuge in the water trapped beneath. Like the Turnstone, the Wilson's Plover is not built for wading, though compensates for its shortcomings by relentlessly searching the exposed sand flats at low tide. It moves in a series of staccato bursts, making several rapid steps followed by a long pause, a behaviour that presumably allows it to scan for any unwitting animals flushed out by its pattering approach.

Many other bird species have modified bodies that enable them to exploit more fully the hidden assets of the intertidal zone, such as elongated legs or beaks, to facilitate wading or probing deep into the sand. A prime example is the commonly sighted Short-Billed Dowitcher that waits patiently in small flocks for the tide's departure. Despite its name, this stocky wader possesses a remarkably long beak that it uses to rifle through the sediments for those hard-to-reach juicy morsels. Sometimes accompanied by the longer legged Stilt Sandpiper, these flighty aggregations follow the receding waves, exploring the sands

Keen eyes of this feathered fisher survey the surroundings, alert for the slightest movement that may betray a potential meal, with the strong spear-shaped bill always ready to stab at small fish, frogs and lizards. The Green Heron *(Butorides virescens)* may be one of the more common West Indian water birds, but it is still a delight, with its striking plumage and approachable, quirky disposition.

Black-Necked Stilts *(Himantopus mexicanus)* congregate in a small pond on Salt Cay, the irregular depth of which is revealed by the varying length their astonishing legs are exposed. These birds often flock together in the early part of the year, but the larger groups gradually break up into breeding pairs. They make their nests directly on the ground and eagerly defend them, not only from intruders but also from rising water levels, by building fortifications with mud.

as untapped areas are abandoned by the retreating waters. In a division of resources governed by size, the much larger American Oystercatcher is able to wade deeper into the sea than its smaller relatives, accessing the more reclusive inhabitants of the sand with its sizeable bill. But the local prize for the longest leg-to-body-size ratio must surely go to the Black-Necked Stilt, a striking pied bird that balances upon a set of exceptionally long, spindly legs. Unable to tuck in their exaggerated undercarriage during flight, they trail their legs behind like pink streamers that only spring into life as the birds prepare to land. Although they have long, straight bills, these are quite delicate and stiletto-like and clearly not designed for probing coarse sands. They are, in fact, used in conjunction with the birds' long necks to stab at more mobile prey that swim within the shallows.

Any specks of land that rise above the sea can become a resting place for the multitude of marine birds that plunder the oceans for their stocks of fish. In this regard the Turks & Caicos are no exception, playing host to many feathered seafarers. Several migratory species use the islands simply as a stopover, a welcome respite to ease their tired wings before continuing their ceaseless travels, while others are longer guests, either using the land as a permanent base, or forming colonies that last as long as their breeding season. The most obvious examples of the latter are the terns, with several species, including Brown Noddies, Sooty, Bridled and Sandwich Terns, assembling in large groups on some of the outlying cays. These noisy congregations usually occur during the summer months and are valiantly defended by all participants. Any uninvited guests are first warned by a series of swooping near misses, which, if unheeded, are followed up with painful pecks from sharp tern beaks.

For all their bravado, these little birds are the epitome of grace, providing a wonderful spectacle in the mere act of feeding. Like a kingfisher of the sea, a tern hovers with rapid wing beats, using slight movements of its body and tail to keep its head motionless and its beak pointing downwards in the form of a rock-steady

dagger. Once locked onto its prey, it drops like a stone, plunging into the water and invariably rising to the surface with a fish grasped within its beak. Before it can return to its roost, however, it often has to run the gauntlet presented by the Magnificent Frigatebirds. These large, black mariners never alight on the water and, rather than fishing for themselves, prefer to use their superb flying abilities to wage a war of aerobatic piracy on other more active fishers. Known as 'klepto-parasites', they steal the food from other birds by launching a series of mid-air attacks until the unfortunate subject of their attention disgorges its latest hard-earned meal. But, as with most bullies, they tend to pick on smaller foe and are therefore unlikely to bother the island's only resident large bird of prey, the Osprey. Feeding exclusively on fish, this sea hawk can regularly be seen flying over the coastal seas, cruising far above the water level. They fly with deep, determined wing beats, pausing every so often to glide on the air beneath their broad wingspans. When an individual's keen eyesight spies a fish near the surface, the bird plummets seaward, crashing into the water feet first to grasp with long, curved talons

A Sooty Tern *(Sterna fuscata)* gently alights on a convenient rock on one of the outlying cays. Here they form breeding colonies with other tern species, especially the similar looking Bridled Tern *(Sterna anaethetus)*, as well as Brown Noddies *(Anous stolidus)*. Each pair only ever produces a single, speckled egg, which on these bird islands is laid directly on the ground amongst the scattered bones of small fish.

its slippery prey. Making an immediate take-off to prevent its feathers from becoming waterlogged, it propels itself from the churning foam, sometimes having to fight with its writhing burden as it lopes ever skyward. Unable to feed on the wing, it returns to a roost to eat its freshly caught meal, or flies back to its partner, if chicks need to be fed. In contrast to its majestic appearance, the Osprey's nest is a somewhat untidy affair, a large, messy heap of driftwood and other flotsam constructed on a rocky promontory or simply piled on the ground in some of the more remote cays. Pairs tend to use the same nest each year, adding more fragments to their shambling edifice and signifying their return with plaintive whistling cries that carry across the waves.

As with the Osprey and terns, many other seabirds catch fish by diving into the water, though one species deserves a special mention: the Brown Pelican. When flying, their huge beaks and large heads are sunk back into their shoulders, accentuating their top-heavy appearance and somehow giving the impression of a prehistoric throwback, perhaps our modern-day pterodactyls.

An Osprey *(Pandion haliaetus)* takes advantage of a deserted Grace Bay beach, Providenciales, to bask in the early morning sunlight. When hunting Ospreys will often hover an appreciable distance above the water, their large eyes providing them with excellent vision and their long hook-like talons ensuring a secure grip. After a successful strike, the bird will invariably hold its often-heavy prey aligned to its own body, using the streamlining of the fish to reduce its considerable drag.

They are often seen in small, single line squadrons which suddenly roll out of formation to crash into the sea, using their capacious bills to scoop up Silversides before straining the water from their under-slung pouch. Though a visit to the Turks & Caicos may represent the first opportunity to see a pelican in the wild, their characteristic ungainly shape will be remembered by many from childhood books. The same can be said for another local bird, the Flamingo, which features heavily in fables, from Alice in Wonderland to tales about the Phoenix. Usually seen further inland around saltwater ponds, the birds' vivid pink coloration creates a dazzling wash above the water that shimmers in the heat of the midday sun. Compared to their parents, the juvenile birds have a rather drab attire composed mainly of grey and white feathers. Their rosy complexion comes with age as red pigments obtained from their diet gradually accumulate in their plumage. Being the only birds known to filter feed, they use their peculiar but highly modified beaks to sieve out the tiny organisms that live in the saline mud, pumping the water through with rapid movements of their tongues.

Juveniles of the Greater Flamingo *(Phoenicopterus ruber)* lack the striking pink plumage of their parents. For all their imposing size, these birds are remarkably timid and naturally gregarious, to such an extent that if the numbers in a flock are too small they will often fail to breed.

Herons are a common sight throughout the islands as the abundant saltwater ponds provide a plentiful food supply for these wading birds. But, unlike the Yellow-Crowned Night-Heron *(Nyctanassa violacea)* that hunts for crabs and the long-legged Tricoloured Heron *(Hydranassa tricolor)* that can wade into deep water in search of its prey, the Cattle Egret *(Bubulcus ibis)* is almost always found inland feeding on insects disturbed by cattle and horses.

Downy feathers still cover the head of this juvenile Green Heron *(Butorides virescens)*, which, combined with its over-sized feet and bill, give it a rather helpless appearance. The young birds are much paler than the adults, having streaky white underparts and lacking the black crest and chestnut-coloured neck that only develops as they reach maturity. Unlike most other herons, they neither roost nor nest in colonies and prefer the isolation of dense mangrove stands.

Even when hundreds of flamingos form a 'pat' that extends across a lagoon, they present little competition to the numerous egrets and herons that can often accompany them at the edge of the ponds. Hunting small fish and invertebrates, these keen-eyed birds stalk the shallow inland waters, using their snake-like necks to stab long beaks in the direction of their prey. All the North American species have managed to find their way to the Turks & Caicos, their sizes ranging from the Great Blue Heron that stands almost as tall as the flamingos, to the petite Green Heron and much rarer Least Bittern. Most rely on their fishing abilities to provide them with food, but the Cattle Egret prefers to hunt on land, collecting insects as the main part of its diet. During the breeding season they can be readily distinguished from the other white herons by a glorious gold to orange crest, with the colour also appearing on their shoulders and chest. Although they strut around the low-lying vegetation with an arrogant air, pecking at the tiny creatures that buzz by, their direct chasing abilities are insignificant when compared to the Grey Kingbird.

Grey Kingbirds *(Tyrannus dominicensis)* and their close relatives are found exclusively in the New World, where they are renowned for their belligerent and aggressive defence of their territory. These birds will take on all intruders and, although they rarely hit people, their attacks will often dislodge feathers from birds as big as Ospreys. They reign over the islands during the summer months when they visit from the south-eastern Caribbean in order to breed.

Flicking its long, black and white tail in a characteristic sideways motion, a little Blue-Grey Gnatcatcher *(Polioptila caerulea)* peers out from behind what appear to be white-rimmed spectacles. Like the Grey Kingbird, this species can be described as a flycatcher, but instead of chasing large bugs through the air, the gnatcatcher tends to remain amongst the shrubbery, working its way through the foliage and gleaning insects from the leaf surfaces and along the branches.

Sitting on lookout posts these birds noisily proclaim their presence, making frequent sorties to catch large insects on the wing before flying back to their perches to beat them into submission. They are very territorial and openly aggressive, hurling verbal abuse at any trespassers before and after making swooping attacks. Continuously communicating, breeding pairs will hail one another as they meet and, as they often share the same perch, this can be a very common occurrence. Despite their incessant calling, their voices are no match for one bird that can be found amongst the tall trees of the Caicos Islands. At first one may be fooled into thinking that some species of parrot is proclaiming its territory, with deafening shrieks and squawks echoing out across the treetops. However, a closer inspection will reveal only a few black crows and the temptation may be to continue searching for a more brightly coloured companion amongst the leaves. But these inconspicuous Cuban Crows are the source of the cacophony, each bird belting out a succession of amazing sounds that are punctuated by low guttural jabberings.

Although none are able to compete with the resonance achieved by the 'song' of the Cuban Crow, many of the islands' birds produce quite melodious tunes. The tiny Blue-Grey Gnatcatcher is easily approached as it hops through the lower branches of small bushes, tolerating our presence with only a few scolding chirps. But it may regale the lucky bystander with a prolonged

In spite of their name, Cuban Crows *(Corvus nasicus)* are residents here, ranging from Provo to East Caicos. Their appearance and sound are unmistakable, being the only crows found in the islands and ones that produce an incredibly loud, raucous call. Common in the dense woodland around Kew, North Caicos, they are often seen skulking around the playground of the local school, apparently using teamwork to steal food from the children.

performance of a twittering song, its pair of white eye-rings looking like the stage makeup of some operatic artist. Holding its relatively long tail in a pose that resembles a wren, it picks off small insects from amongst the foliage. While watching this pretty little bird skip about its business it may be difficult to believe that the Turks & Caicos are home to an even smaller species, but the Bahama Woodstar is just a fraction of its length, at a mere three and a half inches long. First encounters are usually a whirring flypast at lightning speed more reminiscent of

The iridescent throat patch of the male Bahama Woodstar *(Calliphlox evelynae)* appears black when seen from an unfavourable angle as its spectacular colours are created simply by sunlight reflecting off its feathers. As their name suggests, these delightful hummingbirds occur throughout the Bahamas chain, but a locally distinct race does exist in the Inaguas where the violet feathers of the male also extend further up onto its forehead.

Although not officially recorded for the Turks & Caicos, this young White Ibis *(Eudocimus albus)* stands in the shallow waters of a salina on Salt Cay, unaware of its misdemeanour. While relatively common in Florida, these birds are only rare vagrants in the Bahamas and this young individual may have simply strayed off course. The species is named after the adult's plumage, which is pure white, except for the glossy black wing tips that remain concealed when the bird is at rest.

a large bee on steroids than of a bird. However, the blurred flight path comes to an abrupt end in front of the nearest bloom, as this little green-backed hummingbird pauses for a drink of nectar. Using its needle-like bill to probe the flowers, it hovers back and forth with amazing agility, its tiny wings beating so fast they almost become invisible. These birds tend to use an isolated twig as a perch and this provides the best opportunity to observe them in their full glory. The male is the more striking of the sexes, possessing an iridescent violet throat patch that flashes breathtaking colours as it reflects the tropical sunlight, earning its alternative name of the God Bird.

The simple fact that birds can fly has allowed many to populate the far-flung islands of the Turks & Caicos. Several species make only fleeting appearances, some taking planned refuelling stops along the route of their annual migrations, while others are simply blown off course by adverse weather conditions. But the transient nature of these aerial visitors has been a vital part of the eventual greening of the exposed reefs, because they often bring with them a variety of seeds that act as floral time capsules from distant lands.

Floral Survivors

The life and death struggle of the reef, coupled with the constant pounding by the vast Atlantic Ocean and the eroding activities of a million marine organisms result in an endless supply of limestone sediments that shift and swirl with the water currents flowing over the banks. Before sea level changes provided added height to the land, water movements would accumulate these white sands to an extent where they started to rise above the sea, forming a small cay. The production of similar embryonic islands can still be observed today, but, by their very nature, they tend to be short-lived and vulnerable to being destroyed by stormy weather. However, they provide a resting-place for passing birds, which often leave behind botanical hitchhikers. Many seeds are modified to secure a ride, either attached to the outside with hooks or glue, or travelling safely enclosed within the bird's gut. If conditions are right, a new arrival can germinate and subsequently attempt to consolidate the virginal territory, but the odds are by no means in its favour. The sands are often impregnated with a great deal of salt, which contrasts markedly with the relatively few nutrients and, if the juvenile plant is to survive past a few days, rain must fall soon. Below the waves, the sands are often stabilised by seagrass meadows and mangroves may colonise the periphery, but before the land can be transformed any further, birds are often required to perform an additional service. The fertilising properties of seabird droppings have long been recognised by man in the mining and use of guano and, if birds continue to frequent the developing island, their dietary deposits can make the sands more hospitable for any subsequent seedlings.

Other than as air cargo, many seeds arrive as flotsam, washed ashore and unceremoniously dumped amongst the other debris that make up the strandline. From these humble beginnings many beautiful creations can spawn, like the Beach Morning Glory, which creeps its way up the sand and spreads out to cover the dunes above the high water mark, bearing flowers like vibrant pink trumpets. Whilst humans – with their sunscreen and refreshing cocktails – may consider this new home a tropical paradise, for a plant it is an extremely harsh environment. During the heat of the day, when the sun relentlessly bakes the

Clusters of impressive spines protect the plump stems and red flower buds of the Prickly Pear cactus *(Opuntia dillenii)*. It is a common misconception that cacti are restricted to deserts; in fact only a few are able to grow in such harsh environments and most live in warm, dry climates where water loss must be controlled. Many species have large, impressive flowers that will often open only at night.

earth, animals have the capacity to move into burrows or rest within some shaded recess, avoiding the dehydrating effects of the oven-like atmosphere. However, plants are literally rooted to the spot, unable to evade adverse conditions, and for many, unable to grow in a shady location as they need good light to photosynthesise.

Coupled with high temperatures, the Turks & Caicos receive little rainfall and what does descend from the skies quickly drains away. Therefore only very resilient, highly adapted organisms can stand proud upon the dry, sandy earth, surviving all that Mother Nature can deliver for long enough to create a further generation. For this reason most of the native flora are classed as 'xerophytes', plants that can cope with living in dry or desert-like regions. In one way or another, their bodies are adapted to conserve water, for without this precious resource they will eventually die. The Turks Head Cactus is a fine example of a local xerophyte that has great relevance to the Turks & Caicos, for it is the namesake of the Turks Islands and has been depicted on the nation's flag and coat of arms. On the top of its rotund spiny body, this cactus sports a pad of crimson red bristles that

Namesake of the Turks Islands, the Turks Head Cactus *(Melocactus intortus)* may be a common sight here, but the plant is not restricted to these shores. Its range encompasses many of the drier West Indian islands and this rather portly-shaped species was first described in 1768 using specimens collected from Antigua. The red coloured 'fez' is formed by tightly packed spines and bears the small pink flowers when the plant finally matures.

often resembles a Turkish fez, presumably the origin of its common name. Everything about the plant is geared for water collection and conservation, with the thick fleshy stem being packed with water storage cells to allow the plant to survive times of prolonged drought, and the tough waxy cuticle helping to seal in any acquired water. Even the plant's shape is important, with the barrel-like appearance of the stem limiting the surface area, effectively reducing the regions where evaporation can occur. Although the heavy ridges down the sides may seem to counter this adaptation, they too are thought to have a significant role, reducing the tissue damage caused by shrinkage, which is an inevitable consequence of the internal water being used up while the plant waits for the next rains.

One of the most obvious characteristics of flowering plants is their leaves, which are essentially solar panels that facilitate the energy production needed for life. To do an efficient job, a leaf usually has a large surface area, but, where water is the limiting factor, lush foliage is a luxury that would soon lead to the plant's

Beach Morning Glory *(Ipomoea pes-caprae)* is a true pioneering mariner since its seeds can germinate in seawater, which has led to its presence on tropical coastlines world-wide. Once a seedling is washed ashore, vine-like creepers spread out across the sand using a host of adventitious roots to consolidate its sandy territory. Its beautiful pink blooms disguise the fact that large areas are eventually smothered, with little regard for the vanquished species below.

Several egg-shaped, red fruits seem a heavy burden for this
Prickly Pear *(Opuntia dillenii)*, which clings to its existence
on a craggy limestone cliff. But this species is a true
survivor, being an abundant native of the islands and often
becoming a pest in other areas of the world where it has
been introduced. In fact, cacti have only existed outside the
Americas since the first European explorers took them
home as curios.

demise. Therefore, as an arid climate adaptation, the leaves of many xerophytes have been greatly reduced to form spines, while the role of photosynthesis has been taken on by the stem itself. The spines have a clear role in defence, jealously guarding the plant's stored water from passing animal admirers, but they also have several less obvious functions. Being dry structures, they serve to increase the plant's surface area for heat loss without the consequence of water loss associated with fleshy tissues. In addition, their light colour helps to reflect the heat, while their pointed shape can concentrate airborne moisture into droplets that fall onto the ground to be picked up by the roots. Although some species of cacti form large underground tubers for water storage, or produce deep tap roots, the relatively thin soils and limited groundwater in the Turks & Caicos mean that the majority living here have fine, widespread root systems. These complex nets only penetrate the ground for a short distance, but they cover huge areas so the slightest rainfall can be caught and stored with the greatest efficiency.

Waxy outer surfaces and thick, swollen stems are general characteristics of cacti, like this Bearded Cactus *(Cephalocereus* sp.*)*, which improve the plant's ability to store water. Although these features provide an obvious advantage when living in dry conditions, the same attributes aid plants that grow near saltwater, with the succulent leaves of the Seaside Samphire *(Sesuvium portulacastrum)* taking on the same role as the cactus stem.

Cacti are not the only plants able to withstand dry conditions. Bromeliads are another New World group of xerophytes, the most famous being the pineapple, but the majority are small, existing as epiphytes growing on the branches of trees. Here, the Twisted & Banded Airplant *(Tillandsia flexuosa)* simply uses its roots as an attachment, with water being collected in the cup-shaped spiral of leaves, from which the spindly flower stalk eventually arises.

Lying prostrate on the windward shore of East Caicos, a West Indian Laurel *(Calophyllum antillanum)* seems to have been squashed by a giant hand. The trunk and branches twist and creep like a vine across the rocks, while the foliage that would normally be held aloft, more closely resembles a stunted shrub. The tree has grown this way as a result of the prevailing easterlies that often whip off the Atlantic onto this exposed coast heavily laden with salty sea spray.

One of the most impressive adaptations found in plants like the Turks Head Cactus is their method of photosynthesis. Other than water and light, carbon dioxide is a required ingredient for this process and it is readily found within the atmosphere. To allow this gas inside their bodies, plants have microscopic openings called 'stomata' that can be opened and closed dependant on their requirements and the ambient conditions. But this causes a problem for desert dwellers, as when the stomata are opened to take in air, the protective barrier of their waxy cuticle is breached and water can readily evaporate from the succulent internal tissues. To limit this problem the stomata are found in pits, which become filled with humid air, so reducing evaporation. The hairs and spines of cacti also help in this concern by breaking up and slowing the air movements just above their surfaces, providing a layer of humidity like a force field around the plant. But these slight structural modifications pale into insignificance when considering that the stomata of cacti only open during the night, when the cool air results in less evaporation. Most plants would be unable to do this, as the lack of light associated with the nocturnal hours would prevent photosynthesis. However, the desert dwellers have an ingenious solution, whereby the carbon dioxide they absorb under the cover of darkness is converted into an organic compound. As dawn approaches the stomata are closed, raising the fortifi-

cations against the rising sun, while safe within the ramparts the carbon dioxide is slowly released from storage, allowing self-contained photosynthesis to occur throughout the day.

With many of the islands of this archipelago being quite small, the surrounding seas undeniably influence the vegetation. Anyone who has lived near the coast and owned a car will understand the destructive effects of the salt-laden sea breezes, with the bodywork of their pride and joy seeming to rust faster

Sea Grape *(Coccoloba uvifera)* is a native plant of the West Indies and is common throughout the Turks & Caicos. As its name suggests, this shrub is often found on or near the seashore, but further inland it can grow to a considerable height. Each plant is either male or female and when the grape-like fruits are ripe they turn reddish-purple and can make an excellent jam.

than it can be polished. The same can be said for many land plants that eke out an existence close to the breaking waves, the briny air damaging exposed tissues, often resulting in rust coloured marks on their leaves. Their growth is also stunted, with species that usually form large bushes, such as the Sea Grape, occurring as flattened shrubs that appear to cower close to the ground in deference to the power of the nearby sea. In areas where the soil has become highly saline, resistant specialists find their niche. Herbaceous plants like Seaside Samphire can form extensive mats that cover large areas of affected ground and from a distance this succulent carpet can look like a carefully manicured lawn. Another salt-tolerant species is the Buttonwood, a tree that is sometimes mistaken for a mangrove as they are often found along the landward side of these more specialised plants.

One tree that usually grows just beyond the strandline is the Casuarina, a tall pine that lines the beaches in apparent defiance of the encroaching waters. Like the xerophytes, pine trees are well adapted to conditions where freshwater is limited, albeit more usually when it is locked within snow and ice. But unlike the native plants, whose seeds were delivered by natural processes, the presence of this species in the Caribbean has resulted from human intervention. More commonly known as the Australian

Both the yellow-flowered Miraculous Vine *(Momordica charantia)* and the Orange Geiger Tree *(Cordia sebestena)* are native Caribbean plants that are reputed to have many medicinal properties. Though the red seeds are considered poisonous, the leaves of the vine make a tea for treating ailments that range from flu to diabetes. On the other hand, all parts of the Geiger Tree seem to be used in some form of herbal remedy, from alleviating breathing difficulties to soothing insect bites.

The rather delicate looking Spider Lily *(Hymenocallis sp.)* is a
native West Indian plant that prefers coastal locations, but
here the low rainfall tends to restrict its existence to select
areas cared for by a keen gardener. The shape of its flowers
may seem oddly familiar and it is the white trumpet-like
cup, formed by the webbing that joins yellow-tipped
stamens, that betrays its close relationship to the daffodil.

Glossy, green foliage and an array of slender, funnel-shaped flowers make the native American Yellow Oleander *(Thevetia peruviana)* an attractive addition to any tropical garden. However, behind the plant's aesthetic appeal there lies a poisoned chalice. From the beautiful flowers to the tips of the roots, all the tissues are highly toxic, this plant having developed extremely powerful defences against unwelcome herbivores.

Pine, a name that reveals its true origins, this tree has leaves that occur as tiny scales on long, slender jointed branches, offering another solution to water conservation. With human habitation of these islands and the disposition of our species to tame and cultivate our surroundings, it is not surprising that many of the seemingly natural resident plants of the Turks & Caicos are actually exotic imports. Several have become naturally self-seeding since their introduction and now survive without any further assistance. Common plants like the Rosy Periwinkle, the Giant Milkweed and the Tamarind Tree all have Old World origins, but can now be found rubbing shoulders with the native flora. The conditions in which these foreign additions evolved have furnished them with sufficient adaptations to deal with this harsh terrestrial environment. Conversely, many of the more spectacular introduced species require constant attention to ensure their continued survival. Hibiscus, Spider Lilies and Palm Trees are usually only found within well-tended gardens as they are ill-suited to an arid climate. The local skies by no means satisfy their thirst for water and the enhanced supplies they do receive quickly flow away from their roots, descending through the porous limestone bedrock that is riddled with extensive cave systems.

The Sea~spawned Landscape

The Caicos Islands form a graceful curve that traces the northern boundary of the huge limestone bank from which they rise. The exposed semicircle of main islands starts with West Caicos and is followed by Providenciales, North Caicos, Middle, East and finally South Caicos. Like the beads of a rosary, smaller islands are dotted in between, notably Water, Pine, Parrot and Plandon Cays. The relatively flat expanse of the bank slopes into deeper waters towards the south and therefore few islands are found in this region, except for French Cay to the west and a string of small islands on the eastern edge. This latter chain, from Long Cay off South Caicos down to Bush Cay, follows the sweep of the Columbus Passage, a deep-water trench that separates the Caicos Bank from the adjacent Turks Bank. Scattered across this second submerged plateau reside the Turks Islands, the biggest being Grand Turk and Salt Cay, with eight other minor rocky outcrops surfacing above the waters.

The vast majority of the land is low-lying and incredibly flat, with just the larger islands possessing ridges and hills, the highest point a mere 163 feet above sea level. Indeed, when sailing off the islands it is surprising how soon they disappear from view; their presence only revealed by the reflection of the shallow waters painting the underside of passing clouds a faint turquoise hue. Being formed from soft limestone rock, the exposed edges of the islands are relatively quickly weathered by the action of the tireless waves. Deep undercuts are often carved into the cliffs, an effect that can leave some of the smaller cays resembling mushrooms at low tide. But this erosive power pales into insignificance when compared to the strength wielded by the infrequent rains. Freshwater alone has little effect on limestone, but before the rain seeps down through the porous rock it passes through decaying organic matter that causes it to become acidic, subsequently etching its path through the islands' foundations. But this is by no means the limit of its power. As the rain percolates through the rock it eventually reaches the level of the sea, which extends through all the islands as saline groundwater. Rather than simply flowing into the saltwater, the less dense rainwater floats on top, eventually forming a massive freshwater globule, or lens, within the rock. This phenomenon is more pronounced on the larger

Unusual rock formations decorate the edge of this Middle Caicos sea cliff. At first glance it appears as if the rock itself has melted from above, but undoubtedly these shapes were formed by water dripping within a cave that has since collapsed, or been weathered away by the action of the waves. Marine fossils are often embedded in the limestone that makes up the land, a fact that proves its sea-spawned origin.

Overhangs, such as this, may look impressive but the constant pounding of the sea weakens the rock, eventually causing it to collapse. For the life span of a bird, however, the cliffs represent a safe and secure home. The intricate nature of the limestone gives plenty of resting places for the Brown Noddy *(Anous stolidus)*, which prefers to pluck fish from the water's surface rather than diving for them, like most other terns.

islands, which consequently can support a greater variety of vegetation, with some species being able to tap into this hidden water reserve. At the interface between the lens and the groundwater, slight mixing creates a chemically complex brackish zone that has a much greater capacity for dissolving limestone than either of its parent fluids. This sets the scene for rapid cave development, with the flow of the brackish water gouging out huge caverns and gullies, geologically a fast process, but one that still required many millennia.

The same changes in sea level that unveiled the islands also had the effect of draining some of these flooded caves, exposing the complex system of chambers, tunnels and vaults. The acidified rainwater continued to percolate through the porous limestone, but upon encountering the now air-filled caverns it steadily dripped down from the domed ceilings. As each droplet formed, the air in the cave caused a minute amount of the calcium carbonate, which had become dissolved in this weak acid, to be deposited on the roof of the cave. In a similar fashion, when the water splashed onto the cave floor, more carbonate was

A green canopy stretches out across North Caicos to the distant waters of the Caicos Bank. This relatively lush vegetation is in stark contrast to the parched flora found on the smaller islands and can be attributed to a trapped freshwater supply lying within the porous rock of this larger landmass. The presence of the trees also helps to maintain water within the system and is thought to induce a higher local rainfall that replenishes the moisture used by the plants.

Bats are the only native terrestrial mammals of the Turks & Caicos and presumably made their way to the islands in the same manner as the resident bird population, with wayward individuals being blown off course. But rather than island-hopping down the Bahamas chain from mainland America, they are probably descended from bats that originated from Cuba or Hispaniola, as they more closely resemble the species found in the Greater Antilles.

deposited and with the passage of time, the caves began to fill with the characteristic stalactites and stalagmites of more conventionally formed caverns.

Many of the islands have features that testify to the honeycombed nature of their foundations. Easily accessible cave systems can be found on both East and Middle Caicos, with the latter being the most impressive. The main entrance is a long, gaping fissure within the hillside that opens out into a cavernous maw, complete with fang-like rock projections from above and below. Further smaller openings allow shafts of light to dance on the prehistoric floors, the sun's rays sometimes reflecting off tranquil pools of rainwater, which is still working its magic on the limestone. The natural illumination allows the more adventurous to explore quite some distance into the cave, but as the light dims, an unfamiliar musty smell grows at the same intensity as the soil underfoot. Upon hearing the high-pitched squeaks and fluttering noises from above, realisation dawns on the subterranean wanderer that they have inadvertently stumbled across the cave's healthy bat population. The earthy substance that covers the rocks is many years' worth of bat droppings, an excellent fertiliser that once supported a local guano mine. With the aid of a flashlight, the small flying mammals can be seen congregating within hollows in the ceiling, clinging to the rock

and launching into flight as the artificial beam of light disturbs their rest. With their forearms and hands modified to form wings, their hind legs are used mainly to hold onto the rock, allowing them to hang upside down in repose. Although they may look ungainly, bats have excellent flight musculature that affords them unrivalled aerobatic prowess, a perfect adaptation for manoeuvring within the enclosed spaces of a cave. A further consideration is that all of this aerial agility can be achieved in total darkness, which can be attributed to their amazing powers of echolocation. By producing high-frequency whistles with their voice boxes and listening for the reflected sound waves, they are able to build a 'picture' of their surroundings in much the same way as a radar operates on modern aircraft. A bat's system,

Three species of bats have been found living in
the caves of Middle Caicos: Leach's Long-Tongued
Bat *(Monophyllus redmani)*, the Buffy Flower Bat
(Erophylla sezekorni) and the Antillean Fruit-Eating Bat
(Brachyphylla nana). The latter is the largest found anywhere
in the islands, but is still quite small, having a wingspan
of just twelve inches. Oddly enough, no bats have
ever been recorded for any of the Turks Islands.

Just within a few feet of its narrow entrance, the Conch
Bar Caves of Middle Caicos open out into a most
impressive spectacle of limestone architecture. Thick
columns support the high ceiling, the downward spreading
stalactites having fused with their upwardly mobile
stalagmite counterparts, while the cave's floor is a jumbled
expanse of large boulders, littered with perfectly still,
crystal-clear pools.

however, is so accurate that it can not only detect insects as tiny
as mosquitoes, but it can also catch one in its mouth while on
the wing. Two of the six species of bats found in the Turks &
Caicos feed on insects in this way, while the others are all
vegetarians, relying on fruit, pollen and nectar to provide their
active little bodies with enough energy. As for other inhabitants
of the caves, owls have been known to roost on the ledges, but
these feathered nocturnal hunters are much more elusive than
their flighty mammalian counterparts.

Although the sunlit area near the entrance of the caves on
Middle Caicos can be safely explored, towards the back several

rooms and tunnels lead off into the gloom. A journey into these
recesses would be foolhardy without the aid of flashlights and
the knowledge of an experienced local guide, for this cave system
is one of the most extensive in the whole of the Greater
Caribbean. One feature that makes the caverns so complex is
that the changing sea level has produced numerous layers of
caves, the rocks resembling a multi-storey carpark with several
passageways linking the different floors. To what depth this
system extends is unknown, but, with the lower storeys flooded
by the saline ground water, it is certainly in excess of 200 feet
below the current sea level. This estimate is based on depth
soundings of the nearby Ocean Hole, located off the southern

coast of Middle Caicos. This foreboding dark blue circle, surrounded by the lighter coloured shallows, is more than 400 yards across and was produced when the roof of a huge cavern collapsed under its own weight. Many myths and prophecies of doom surround its dark, eerie waters, with sightings of odd-looking fish having been reported by those who have dared to dive below the surface. However, for the most part, like the rest of the islands' underwater cave systems, its secrets still await discovery.

Either the collapse of a roof or the constant surging of waves probably caused the formation of another local feature, 'The Hole', on Providenciales. This sheer-walled crater is over forty feet wide with a base that descends well below sea level. As a result, the lower reaches are filled with water and although they can be approached via a small tunnel to the side, the downward journey is a little unsafe and an easy exit is never guaranteed.

Yawning like the mouth of some mythical beast, The Hole probably resulted from the roof of an ancient cave collapsing. With such dark recesses being a perfect setting for spooky tales, one local nocturnal bird sometimes inhabits the caves and is sure to have elicited many a ghost story. Even the most intrepid explorer is likely to jump when confronted with the white glaring face of a Barn Owl *(Tyto alba)*, coupled with its most unbird-like scream of a call.

Areas of more accessible water abound throughout the islands, but most of the lakes and ponds are filled with saltwater, either being directly connected to the sea through inlets, or formed in areas where the underlying limestone is below sea level. Sometimes the saline groundwater bubbles up through natural sinkholes connected to the submerged cave systems below, with a fine example, the Boiling Hole, being found on South Caicos. On other islands, the borders of large lakes, such as Flamingo Pond on North Caicos, fluctuate with the rise and fall of the tide. Fiddler Crabs and Stocky Ceriths can be seen on the muddy banks, oblivious to the irony of marine species living as far from the sea as these islands will allow. But other true terrestrial animals can be found nearby, either basking in the sun, or rustling through the undergrowth, roaming the lands where their ancestors were once washed ashore.

Rather uninviting lime-green water awaits those reckless enough to jump into The Hole, Providenciales. Many other clearer, more picturesque ponds and lakes occur within the islands, most being shallow areas of saltwater that have seeped up through the perforated bedrock. Lake Catherine on West Caicos is a perfect example, where cerith molluscs teem in its sheltered depths and flamingos wade across its still expanse.

A Collection of Castaways

After the islands, as it were, rose from the sea, the arrival of land animals may be presumed to have progressed in an orderly fashion, requiring the initial establishment of plants, before herbivores, followed by predators, could begin their colonisation. This classic succession, however, is not always the case on small coral islands, which are often able to support a variety of animal life in the absence of any vegetation. Scavengers that arrive clinging to floating debris would certainly have a plentiful supply of food, brought by the tide in the form of dead or dying sea creatures. The ultimate source of this nourishment would be the marine plants within the nearby seas, but the scavengers would in turn become tasty morsels for any predatory castaways, adding an extra tier to this simple food chain. With the eventual arrival of plants, the needs of herbivores could be met, but continued survival requires much more than a few bites to eat. Just as the germinating plants that spread their tendrils over the land require water, so too do the beasts that walk the dry sands. Most plunder the reserves of other organisms, deriving enough fluids from their diet, though water conservation is still of utmost concern. But, whether any of these natural Robinson Crusoes can survive for a few days, or perhaps years, is irrelevant with respect to its species becoming established. Unless chance delivers a compatible partner to these restricted shores, its presence will be doomed to extinction, a hapless visitor without the hope of a rescue sailing into view.

Even if an individual manages to win the lottery of finding a mate and can adequately cope with the everyday rigours to breed successfully, islands are inherently changeable environments and extinctions are common occurrences. Sea level changes and severe weather can result in the land disappearing altogether, its inhabitants washed away by the churning seas. On a similar note, the smaller the land mass the less likely protected areas, such as valleys and gullies, will be available as refuges, leaving nowhere to shelter from exceptionally harsh conditions. In addition, small

Iguanas were presumably among the first animals to become established on these islands, since they must have been isolated for a great deal of time to enable a distinct species, the Turks & Caicos Rock Iguana *(Cyclura carinata)*, to evolve. Compared to other West Indian iguanas, their population is considered quite healthy, but they are still critically endangered and their fate remains in the balance.

populations are simply more vulnerable to the vagaries of chance, with a poor breeding season, or the loss of a mate heralding the end of a lineage. Perhaps most surprising is the consideration that the right type of predator may not be present. With armaments and defences evolved for foreign climes, a particular animal may prove to be invincible within its new habitat. Such an imbalance may result in a population explosion that leads to the complete consumption of the available food and the species' inevitable demise.

The seclusion of far-flung islands is often portrayed as a blank slate for the processes of evolution, which accounts for their high proportion of endemic, or unique, species. Organisms that arrive on their shores are free to exploit the available food sources and natural selection favours those best suited to cope or able to adapt. But the exposed rocks of the Turks & Caicos are estimated to be less than 150 000 years old and this period is simply not long enough for, say, local marine snails to evolve into air breathing forms. The land snails that litter the ground and congregate on shady branches have all evolved elsewhere from their aquatic ancestors and have been transported to these

Safe within the shade of a furled leaf, a land snail waits for the cover of darkness before exposing its soft tissues to the drying air. The Manchineel tree *(Hippomane mancinella)* this mollusc is on affords even more security, as the sap is highly poisonous. For some small invertebrates, feeding on plants like this often empowers them with their own toxic properties, making them unpalatable or even lethal to potential predators.

Land snails are not renowned for their speed or agility and so when a good food supply has been located it is often worth their while to find a nearby resting place. Unfortunately for this individual, however, it has to spend the daylight hours in a rather exposed position, unable to move for fear of drying up under the tropical sun. The light colour of its shell will help to reflect the heat, but whether it survives to the cool of the evening will depend on the vigilance of the local birdlife.

Water conservation is a primary concern for terrestrial animals, especially when living in a hot, dry climate. For these land snails, the bulk of their water will be acquired through their vegetarian diet, but the moisture they consume must sustain them for as long as possible. By trapping the water within their shells and spending the daylight hours in shaded areas, like this gnarled tree trunk, they can reduce moisture loss through evaporation.

 77

Determining the sex of a mature Turks & Caicos Rock Iguana *(Cyclura carinata)* is a fairly simple task. A female, pictured here, is distinguishable by the relatively smooth ridge that runs down her back, which obviously lacks the long spike-like scales of the masculine crest. Both sexes take around six years to reach maturity and live for an average of fifteen years, although some have been known to reach the grand old age of twenty-five.

islands already equipped to deal with terrestrial life. However, isolation has caused the formation of a few distinct species, with interbreeding populations separated from their parental stock long enough to exaggerate certain characteristics. The largest native animal, the Turks & Caicos Rock Iguana, often exceeds two feet long and is a prime example of such speciation, being related to the iguanas of South America. As with most reptiles, these lizards are often found basking in the sun during the early hours, warming their bodies before their daily exertions. Rather than being a gentle way of easing into the morning, this is a vital ritual to ensure their survival, for these animals are 'ectotherms', gaining their body heat from the surrounding environment. By a series of behavioural and physiological adaptations, they are able to maintain their internal temperature at a relatively constant 98°F (37°C), with the blood of some species being a few degrees hotter. Evidently the term 'cold-blooded' ill-describes such a physique. Although reptiles are unable to live in very cold climates, or adopt a purely nocturnal existence, their food requirements are much less than birds and mammals, which have to burn calories to produce their own body heat. In fact, a reptile only requires ten per cent of the food needed by a mammal of the same size, an obvious advantage for life on a small island. Also, this may explain why the only endemic non-flying vertebrates found in the Turks & Caicos are reptiles, with perhaps the mammals that embarked on involuntary sea journeys succumbing to starvation before being washed ashore.

Once heated by the sun, the Rock Iguanas scuttle about their business, with sinuous movements of their long bodies reminiscent of their distant fish-like ancestors. Although their short legs can propel them through the undergrowth at rapid speeds, their position on the side of the body makes them rather inefficient. Therefore, a resting lizard will invariably lie upon its slightly rotund belly. Protecting their bodies is the scaly reptilian skin, a watertight covering well suited to the arid climate of the Turks & Caicos. Made from a substance similar to our fingernails, these chain-mail suits suffer from everyday wear and

The first few hours of sunlight are often the best time to observe wild Rock Iguanas, as this is when they are generally found out in the open, warming themselves after their slumber. Care must be taken, however, when visiting the cays they inhabit, since these animals spend both the night and the heat of the day within burrows dug using their long claws and unguided wanderings may collapse their subterranean homes.

tear and are shed every so often, being replaced by another from below. The males possess a row of elongated scales along their backbone that form an impressive spiky ridge, giving them a dragon-like appearance. However, despite their fierce looks, these are no fire-breathing monsters, but rather shy and harmless vegetarians eating nothing more sinister than leaves, along with any berries and fruits they can find.

As the sun rises in the sky, the heat needed to warm their bodies now threatens to cook the animals within their impermeable skins. In order to cool themselves, the iguanas seek the shade of

small shrubs, eventually retreating to the sanctuary of their burrows, which they dig to a shallow depth in the thin soils. As the day draws to a close, they once again emerge to soak up the sun's rays, collecting enough warmth to see them through the night before retiring to the controlled environment of their underground dens. The Rock Iguanas reach maturity at around six years of age and after mating, the females bury a small clutch of leathery eggs within a specially-made nesting chamber. Once their offspring are sealed away, the lizard's parental duties are over until the next year and the eggs are left to incubate within the warm sand. About three months later, miniature forms of the

adults hatch out and immediately dig their way to the surface, dashing for cover as soon as they free themselves from their natal grave. Like their marine cousins the sea turtles, this is the point in their life where they are most vulnerable to predation, large keen-eyed birds finding them a relatively easy meal. However, the small size of the young cannot be much of a drawback, as many other diminutive lizard species are part of the Turks & Caicos fauna.

Anole and Curly-Tail Lizards occur throughout the islands and few bushes or rocky outcrops seem to exist without at least one representative. Both belong to the same family as the Rock Iguanas, but, being long-legged insectivores, they look quite different from their much larger herbivorous relatives. Although there are several species of anoles to be found, they are reasonably difficult to identify, all appearing as small, usually brown individuals that have a habit of bobbing their upper bodies, as if engaged in a series of push-ups. This unusual display is their way of proclaiming their territory, which they will defend quite vigorously. The males, however, are able to take their exhibition one step further by unfurling a brightly coloured throat fan, or dewlap, which they wave like a semaphore flag, giving an unexpected flash of brilliance to an otherwise drab little animal. On the other hand, the Curly-Tail Lizards are easily

Anole lizards *(Anolis sp.)* spend most of their time climbing through the foliage of trees and shrubs, hunting out insects and other small creatures on which they feed. There are estimated to be about 340 species of these New World reptiles, with over 130 occurring in the Caribbean. The number of species represented in the Turks & Caicos is uncertain, but most trees, walls and even fly-screens seem to support their own fascinating populations.

Poised and ready for action, a Curly-Tail Lizard
(*Leiocephalus* sp.) searches the nearby rocks with its beady
eyes for any hint of its invertebrate prey. Although, like any
animal, a small lizard needs to eat, being a reptile it must
also regulate its temperature by means of its environment
and remaining within the shade during the heat of the
noonday sun is often just as important as finding a meal.

Both of these anoles are engaged in their head-bobbing display, but neither has been tempted to flash its throat fan for the camera. As a form of territorial aggression and as a way to attract a mate, the bright colour of the dewlap undoubtedly sends a loud message through the undergrowth. However, predators may also pick up the signal and even though females have a similar flap of skin, it is presumably too risky for both sexes to advertise in this way.

For anyone with a phobia about snakes, the Turks & Caicos should hold no fears. Only two species exist here, both of which feed on insects and are rarely seen due to their small size and dull coloration. The Pygmy Boa *(Tropidophis greenwayi)*, shown here basking on a rock, is literally dwarfed by the relatively small flowers of the Rosy Periwinkle *(Catharanthus roseus)* and is certainly in more danger from human attention than we are from any bite it can inflict.

separated from the anoles by their characteristic overturned tails, which bounce over their backs as they run. Looking like large question marks, their tails give them a quizzical air as they scamper across the ground in search of their insect prey.

In addition to lizards, the Turks & Caicos are home to two species of snakes, but unlike the beasts that strike fear into the hearts of many, these local serpents are only harmless insectivores. Of the two, the Pygmy Boa is the most surprising, catching unwary animals by crushing them within coils of its body, even though it is not much larger than a common earthworm. Despite the lack of legs, all the world's snakes are predators; every bone in the spine is linked to the next by a ball and socket joint, providing them with an incredible amount of body flexibility. Powerful muscles and specialised scales on their underside allow them to move silently over the ground, while their eyes are covered by immovable transparent eyelids that give them a mesmerising stare.

It is perhaps not a coincidence that most of the endemic reptiles feed upon insects, as these represent a bountiful food supply. As most of these invertebrates fly, at least as adults, it is little wonder how the majority arrived and spread between the islands, their small bodies being easily blown off course by strong winds. Butterflies, crickets and beetles all occur in abundance here,

both in numbers and species. Other than flying, some may have arrived as grubs within driftwood, or clinging, like the reptiles, to the outside of their makeshift rafts. Regardless of how delicate some may look, they all possess a tough outer skeleton of chitin, which is well suited to a hot, dry climate. Their varieties of form are only equalled by their varied diets, some eating the succulent parts of plants, while others devour their own kind and more specialised ones live as parasites on or within reptiles and birds.

The webs of spiders are also a common sight, strung like jewelled curtains between the supports of adjacent branches. But their arrival in the Turks & Caicos may not have resulted from an

ocean journey, for many of these arachnids have a novel means of dispersal. Often, when the young hatch from their cocoon, they climb to the highest point where they attach one of their first strands of silk. Then, like miniature bungie-jumpers, they throw themselves into the wind, reeling out their silken lifeline until it eventually breaks. Buoyed by the long strand of silk, they can float in the air for many miles, the lucky ones eventually coming to land in their new home. With such a random mode of travel, many of the young spiders perish, often being found high in the atmosphere, their leap of faith never delivering them back to earth.

The flora and fauna of the Turks & Caicos would have been struggling to survive for tens of thousands of years when a new animal washed ashore on the beaches. Unlike all that preceded it, this was a tool-using mammal that actually sought out the land on its own pieces of driftwood, deliberately fashioned for the purposes of sea travel. Avoiding the problems of chance, it arrived as family groups and its inevitable appearance changed forever the natural history of these islands.

Camouflaged amongst the green seedpods of the Miamossi *(Leucaena leucocephela)*, a motionless Katydid *(Phoebolampta excellens)* avoids detection by mimicking a leaf. These stout-bodied grasshoppers have gained their odd name from the courtship 'song' of the males. They produce their 'Katy did, Katy didn't' call by rubbing together their forewings, which are hard and cover their membranous flight wings.

CHAPTER THREE

The Sands of Time

The Dawn of Discovery

With only the recent 'discovery' of the Turks & Caicos as an exotic holiday destination, the uninformed visitor may be excused for believing that these rather remote coral outcrops have until now remained relatively untouched by man. While this may be largely true of their pristine fringing reefs, the islands themselves have had quite a long and chequered history of human exploitation, which over the years has considerably changed the composition of the terrestrial vegetation.

For centuries the seemingly endless expanse of the Atlantic Ocean evoked much trepidation among the early European mariners, who seldom ventured far from the coast for fear of sailing off the edge of the world. It was not until 1492, possibly after reaching Iceland and hearing sagas of the Norseman voyages, that one man contested this conviction, believing that he could sail west across this Sea of Darkness to reach the splendid riches of The East, of Cathay (China) and Cipangu (Japan). His aspirations were to be realised when, after seventy-one days of a momentous voyage, an island was seen gleaming in the early morning moonlight. The New World had been discovered. The date was October 12, the man, Christopher Columbus, and the island lay somewhere in the Bahamas chain, though which one exactly is still shrouded in mystery. To date, nine different islands have been claimed as this historic site, with the most popular contenders being Samana Cay, Watling Island and, more recently, Grand Turk.

Columbus named the island San Salvador, which he formally claimed for Spain, but he was far from the first to discover this exquisite land. As the small Spanish flotilla approached the shore, peaceful Indians rushed out onto the white sandy beaches to greet the revered explorers who had arrived at their beloved Guanahani. The fair-skinned strangers who had 'come down from the sky' were presented with wondrous gifts of exotic fruits, fine spun cotton thread and brightly coloured parrots. The indigenes, in return, were delighted to receive small glass beads that glistened in the sun, an unfamiliar jewel to these friendly people. Yet in spite of its rich offerings, this beautiful island could not satisfy Columbus' Midas-like obsession and so, just two days later, the Spaniards returned to their ships and headed south to continue their quest for gold.

The golden rays of an enchanting sunrise reflect off the waves as they roll onto the sandy shore at Mudjin Harbour, Middle Caicos. From the headland you can look out across the expanse of the Atlantic Ocean and try to imagine the three thousand mile journey the Santa Maria, Nina and Pinta made before Columbus and his men finally reached their first landfall in the New World.

A Sooty Tern *(Sterna fuscata)* perches on a rocky cliff of Six Hill Cays. The Grand Turk landfall theory proposes that Columbus moored his ships in the protected waters of Hawk's Nest Anchorage and it may have been ocean-going birds like these that led the mariners to land. But, as fate would have it, the European settlers brought with them domesticated cats, which now restrict the breeding grounds of the terns to only the most remote cays.

Queen Triggerfish *(Balistes vetula)* are striking and beautiful reef fish, but they are also highly valued as a tasty source of food. Their name is derived from their dorsal spines, the first of which is a long spike that can be locked into an upright position. The fish use this to lodge themselves into crevices, but they can release themselves by pressing a second trigger-like spine. They feed on sea urchins by squirting water at them, bowling them over to reveal their vulnerable undersides.

Sadly, many of the questions concerning Columbus' landfall site might have been answered had it not been for the loss of his original log. One account of his journey that still exists is an abridged 'diario', though much controversy centres on its accuracy and interpretation as it was written by a priest-historian well after Columbus' return. In this journal the landfall site was described as a bean-shaped, low-lying island surrounded by reef, with a good large anchorage to the south. The island itself had very green trees and a large lagoon in the centre, though no freshwater to quench the thirst of the exhausted seafarers. As with all the proposed islands there are arguments for and against Grand Turk. It is highly conceivable, however, that the birds that guided Columbus to land were Sooty Terns that still breed on some of the small rocky cays of the Turks Bank. Maybe his first impression of the New World was the sight of the beautiful turquoise waters that surround these enchanted isles.

While the debate over exactly where Columbus took his first footsteps in the New World may never be solved, our knowledge concerning pre-Columbian occupation of the Turks & Caicos continues to expand as more artefacts are unearthed. The earliest inhabitants of these islands were Arawak Indians known as Tainos, who are believed to have fled their homeland in South America to escape persecution from the ruthless Caribs. Aided by favourable currents and the geographical configuration of the Caribbean islands, these peaceful Indians sought passage north, migrating from the Orinoco delta to the Lesser and Greater Antilles and then eventually to the oceanic Bahamas chain.

Collectively, these islands offered a wealth of natural resources and, as a result, an extensive trading network developed. Compared to the lush rainforests and fertile soils of the volcanic islands to the south, the Turks & Caicos may have yielded limited terrestrial harvests, but the food supplied by the rich coral reefs and virgin shallow banks was in abundance. Turtles, fish and conch provided these early settlers with a high protein diet and sufficient surplus for a healthy trade with tribes on the nearby islands of Hispaniola and Cuba. Iguanas, snakes and

Having paddled across 100 miles of open ocean from the island of Hispaniola, a weary Taino seafarer must have welcomed the sight of the sheltered waters of the Caicos Bank. Here, deeper channels can be seen passing close to Mangrove Island, South Caicos, which have been created by the tidal flow of water during its daily movement to and from the banks.

ground-nesting birds are also known to have featured regularly in the Taino diet, but today these vulnerable animals thrive only on the remote cays. Their decimation may have been a result of over-harvesting, but was more likely the unforeseen consequence of the new European colonists introducing cats to a habitat where they did not belong.

The Tainos who originally came to live in this most distant of island groups were simple hunter-gatherers, whose day-to-day lives revolved around their spiritual beliefs. Intricately carven stone idols (Zemi figurines) and ceremonial wooden seats (duhos) have been recovered from archaeological sites over the years, though their prevalence in the limestone caves suggests that these underground labyrinths were particularly important as places of worship. Less ornamental artefacts, including basic earthenware pots and primitive stone implements, have revealed the whereabouts of past Tainan villages, where conical shaped thatched huts once stood prominently amid the cleared vegetation. The caves too are believed to have served as primitive settlements, though they most probably acted as a safe haven from the furious hurricanes that were regular visitors to this newly discovered land.

Barbados Pride *(Caesalpinia pulcherrima)* is a cherished exhibit in tropical gardens the world over, gracing them with its wonderfully flamboyant flowers. However, this impressive shrub is native to the West Indies and is commonly found both in local gardens and living wild in the islands. Its leaves and flowers are known to have medicinal qualities and may have been used by the Tainos to reduce fevers, in addition to its more obvious decorative purpose.

Trading between the islands of the Greater Caribbean took place using large dugout canoes that could endure the pounding of the ocean waves. A crew of up to forty men would swiftly paddle across the open expanse of cobalt blue, their vessel laden with local produce such as dried conch, crystalline salt and cotton used for making 'hamaca' or sling beds. Arriving at their destination they would exchange their goods for perhaps pottery, tobacco or even rubber, which they used in their games of 'batos' - an ancient form of volleyball. Of course, foreign traders would also visit the Turks & Caicos and numerous items of pottery have been discovered that originated from volcanic islands and the South American mainland, as revealed by their mineral content. In particular, broken pieces of earthenware, or potsherds, excavated from Taino occupation sites on Middleton and Long Cay, near South Caicos, reveal a preponderance of imported ceramics, suggesting a high frequency of trade in this area. Moreover, these sites are central to all the settlements so far discovered and may well have been the first commercial seaports to be developed by the seafaring people of these tropical islands.

Undoubtedly, some of the trees that were hollowed to make the sleek trading canoes originated in the Turks & Caicos, which are understood to have experienced a slightly more temperate climate at that time. Valuable hardwoods such as Lignum Vitae, Bay Cedar and Mahogany were probably once common here, though the sands of time have witnessed their gradual demise. Indeed, the large-trunked species have not been the only casualties; the past need for charcoal may have resulted in smaller stemmed varieties, Ironwood, Palm Trunk Wood and Wild Lime also being felled to be gradually replaced by the Red Mangrove, Prickly Pear and dense scrub seen today. Carbon dating of primitive tools found on Grand Turk indicate that cultivation of this land began long before Columbus' arrival, with cassava, sweet potatoes and cotton being the most likely candidates for subsistence farming.

The markedly curved bill and adapted tongue of the Bananaquit *(Coereba flaveola)* is used to probe the blossoms of shrubs and trees to feed on the sticky, sweet nectar they provide. This brightly coloured bird is native to the Turks & Caicos and is often seen, especially when it finds a suitable perch to recite its long, sibilant song. Its range encompasses most of the Greater Caribbean and several colour variants have developed as a result of geographic isolation on different islands.

Irrespective of whether or not Grand Turk was Guanahani, the Tainos who lived on the Turks & Caicos, as elsewhere in the Bahamas, were eventually discovered by the Spanish, though unfortunately the placid Indians bore the brunt of the encounter. With no gold in sight, the Spaniards were initially quick to leave what they perceived as 'barren' islands in search of richer lands that they subsequently found to the south. However, the sources of their new wealth, such as the pearl

Without question, the Taino Indians used the Conch Bar Caves on Middle Caicos in some capacity, whether as a sacred site or simply as a form of shelter. Unfortunately, the most valuable archaeological evidence of their presence here was probably destroyed towards the end of the nineteenth century, when bat guano was the subject of mining activities. Despite this, several artefacts have been found and the caves are now protected within a National Park.

fishery off Venezuela and the gold mines of Hispaniola, demanded much manpower and they were soon to return, but this time with evil intent. In one of the most wicked acts of oppression ever perpetrated by the Spanish Conquistadors, peaceful Taino Indians were abducted from their settlements in their thousands. Sadly, the protected shallow waters that made South Caicos a nucleus for maritime trade also provided easy access for the Spanish slavers to wreak their havoc. As waves of terror spread throughout the island group, Indians on East and Middle Caicos fled to their sacred caves that had always protected them against the wrath of their evil spirit, 'Huracan', but to no avail. Although dense vegetation often obscured the entrances to the caves, these gentle people were unable to escape persecution forever. It has been estimated that about 40 000 Indians from the Bahamas chain were enslaved, brutally murdered or succumbed to European diseases and by 1513, only twenty-one years after Columbus' historic voyage, the Turks & Caicos archipelago had been entirely denuded of its original settlers.

After the barbaric abduction of the Taino Indians, the Turks & Caicos became an uninhabited Spanish possession, appearing on the early navigation charts of the New World, but generally receiving little interest from the many passers-by, eager to reach the newly discovered riches of the Caribbean. Therefore, the indigenous animals and plants were given time to recover from their previous bout of exploitation, allowing them to return to their untamed state and regain their former natural splendour. Over 150 years elapsed before man returned to these islands to live, with this event marking the next chapter in their colourful history.

Islands of White Gold

In today's world of multinational conglomerates, it is interesting to consider that the tiny Turks & Caicos archipelago once exported a commodity that was of such global significance it helped shape the history of the New World and placed these islands firmly in the international trading arena. The resource behind this lucrative trade was not a precious metal, gem or even a newly discovered plant such as tobacco, but a pure white, glistening crystal that reseeded with every incoming tide – salt. Before the advent of refrigeration, this 'white gold' was highly sought after for preserving fresh meat and fish, which is somewhat paradoxical given that the oceans hold an endless supply in solution. Hence, until the more recent discovery of rich deposits in salt domes deep within the Earth's crust, this mineral was primarily obtained from shallow seawater ponds where salt crystals would naturally form. Of course, factors such as a hot, dry climate and porous underlying bedrock dramatically improved the speed of salt crystallisation and the Turks & Caicos provided the perfect conditions.

Probably more so than any other subsequent exploitation, the salt industry exerted a tremendous effect on the landscape of Grand Turk, Salt Cay and South Caicos, the three principal salt-producing islands. While never having supported lush rainforests, these islands are believed to have been much more densely vegetated in the past. Over the course of time, expansive tracts of low-lying land adjoining the lagoons were cleared of vegetation to serve as large shallow ponds for salt production. In doing so, a natural process was interrupted – the moist, cool air that once covered these wooded areas was replaced with a rising wall of heat that reflected from the crystallised salt, causing any passing clouds to dissipate. Thus, the salt pans are believed to have created their own drier 'microclimate', which enhanced the evaporation process and therefore salt production, but caused the surrounding flora and fauna to experience a very harsh, desert-like environment.

Like vast mirrors, these South Caicos salinas provide a perfect reflection of a picturesque cloud-strewn sky. The island, along with Grand Turk and Salt Cay, has a remarkably flat terrain, which offers little resistance to the breezes that blow off the Atlantic. With such an inexhaustible source of energy, windmills were once used to pump the water between the salinas in an effort to improve salt production.

While historical records tell many stories concerning salt trading, unfortunately little attention was paid to the natural history, leaving us somewhat in the dark as to the vegetation that was cleared to make way for the salt industry. The hardwood trees that were used to make cartwheel hubs, such as Lignum Vitae and Mahogany, probably fell early victim. So too would the mangroves that thrive in the saline waters of the lagoons, as many would undoubtedly have been cleared for efficient use of the salt pans. The birdlife was almost certainly affected, with many species moving on to other islands as their habitat was either destroyed or disturbed by human activities. The surprisingly wary and timid flamingo, a splash of vibrant colour amidst the even-toned landscape, may also have sought refuge elsewhere, as these large conspicuous birds were particularly favoured in the cooking pots of the early settlers.

The Bermudians were the first people to exploit the salt-producing potential of these limestone islands. However, it was not until 1678, ten years after their first endeavours, that they established any settlements here and these dwellings were then only occupied on a seasonal basis. Grand Turk was the first island

A natural frosting of brilliant white salt crystals fringes the edge of a shallow, brine-filled pond. The heat of the tropical sun slowly evaporates the water and eventually 'white gold' begins to form. Animals like the flamingo are well adapted to these conditions, but the light glaring off the salt emphasises the sun overhead and instils an empathy for the slaves forced to work in this harsh environment.

Donkeys are common on all the former salt-producing islands as they were introduced as beasts of burden for the salt industry. Those on Salt Cay are quite approachable, but elsewhere they tend to form small herds that shy away from human contact. However, the raucous braying of these now feral animals still proclaims their presence, often breaking the serenity of the salina landscape.

to be developed, with the rectangular-shaped salt ponds, or salinas, coming to occupy much of the central and southern sectors. Seawater entered these salinas via canals that were built specifically for this purpose. For each salina, wooden windmills were used to pump a continuous stream of salt-laden water through a series of reservoirs and sluice gates, these being interconnected by stone-walled gullies. As the water made its journey from pond to pond, its concentration of dissolved minerals would steadily increase through evaporation, with lime and gypsum being deposited along the way. Eventually, when free of major impurities and too saline to sustain aquatic life, the brine reached saturation level, at which point the pure white halite crystals would settle out and the liquid bittern was drained off. Once crystallised, the salt would be manually raked from the pans, the whole process taking three to four weeks under the scorching sun. Donkeys were then used to transport the salt to the storage sheds, in preparation for its subsequent shipment to diverse destinations around the globe. Indeed, descendants of these working animals can still be seen today, where they roam the arid scrub in search of food much as their wild ancestors once roved the African plains.

With demand exceeding supply, the salt industry on Salt Cay and South Caicos developed in much the same way and collectively, Turks salt quickly gaining an enviable reputation for its purity and fine grain. The salinas on South Caicos, however, were initially based around a natural feature that made them unusual in the saltproducing world. Instead of the saline water reaching the salinas by way of man-made channels, a natural subterranean labyrinth allowed the sea to filter through the limestone rock and emerge through an opening in the heart of the island. On an incoming tide, the water would swirl and bubble as it was forced through the fissure, earning this geological feature the name of the Boiling Hole. With an inventive gate system made to control the ebb and flow of the tide, the walled Boiling Hole stood as a citadel in the centre of the salt fields, the underground

Now protected as an historic building, this old salt shed
situated on the South Caicos seafront waits to receive a
further bout of weathering from a storm rolling in from
the Atlantic. The limestone blocks used in its construction
were almost certainly cut from local quarries and their
dramatically etched surfaces bear testament to the
unceasing forces of nature.

passages of which remain unexplored to this day. One possibility is that the entrance to the flooded cave system exists far offshore, a theory that is supported by a local legend that tells of a child who drowned in the hole and whose body was later found miles away at sea.

While salt may not immediately conjure up images of buccaneers and historic treaties, in times when it was the primary method for preserving food, salt was a valuable commodity. As such, ships came to the Turks & Caicos from both sides of the Atlantic, some interested in fair trade and others with piratical plans. Perhaps of greater significance, though, was that the salt islands themselves were viewed as potential targets and over the years their ownership changed repeatedly as foreign navies came, saw and conquered in pursuit of new wealth. It was not until 1781 that the first permanent settlement was established on Grand Turk, seventy-one years after the Bermudians had recaptured the island from the French and Spanish. Later, at the turn of the nineteenth century, Bermudian salt rakers settled in South Caicos and a small town, Cockburn Harbour, developed on the shores of what is considered to be the finest anchorage in the Turks & Caicos.

With rampant inflation following the start of the American Revolution, the Bermudian settlers discovered a heightened prosperity by trading with Washington's army, even if this did necessitate their sloops running the gauntlet of the Royal Navy blockades. However, their good fortunes were short-lived because it was only a few years later that the French launched an attack on Grand Turk and seized control. A young Captain Horatio Nelson made an unsuccessful attempt to return the island to English rule but it was not until the signing of the 1783 Treaty of Paris that this strategic landfall was reinstated within the British realm.

Although this year marked the end of the bloody battles fought over the ownership of the Turks Islands, the political conflicts

Cockburn Harbour provides an excellent safe anchorage, and in times of storms numerous yachts can be seen moored in the sheltered waters. Throughout the ages this inlet, protected by both Long Cay and Dove Cay, has served as a mariners' haven, from the dugout canoes of the Taino Indians to the huge 'barques' of the salt traders. In fact, ballast stones from the latter vessels can still be found today, littering the sandy floor of the harbour.

The English-built, cast-iron lighthouse has been a fixture
at the northern end of Grand Turk for well over a
century, with the reefs of this area being littered with
the wrecks of unfortunate ships that previously
foundered on its coral outcrops. But, even with today's
advanced technology, these waters still pose a threat to
the modern-day adventurer and great care is needed,
especially when navigating your way to shore.

were to continue for over 100 years, mainly in tune with the salt-dependent economic fluctuations of the island group. By 1850 production had soared and concomitant with this was a boom in sea-faring traffic. But now, after nearly 200 years of delivering a world-acclaimed product, the Turks & Caicos salt industry was facing a real threat to its continued survival. The beautiful fringing coral reefs that provided the limestone origins of the islands and made them so suited to salt production, presented a considerable navigational hazard to the vulnerable merchant vessels. So many cargoes and lives were lost on the infamous North East Reef that traders began to question whether they

should bypass these maritime graveyards altogether. By a twist of fate involving the Governor of Jamaica, who experienced a lucky escape as a passenger on a steamer that ran aground on this reef, a solution was eventually offered. In response to this near-tragedy, funds were secured to purchase a cast-iron lighthouse from England, which was shipped in sections to Grand Turk and assembled on-site in 1852. Although it was originally dimly lit, the construction proved to be sufficient to allay the fears of mariners and, subsequently, to save the industry for another century, though ships continued to be wrecked on this treacherous reef for many more years to come.

Only from the air is it possible to appreciate fully the extent to which the industrious Bermudians modified the landscape of the salt islands. Here the tableau of South Caicos is draped with its patchwork of salinas, some appearing slightly pink owing to the growth of red algae in their shallow waters. Although this area may seem barren and lifeless, with your feet placed firmly on the ground it is easy to find the abundant birdlife and other natural delights that it harbours.

It is perhaps a little ironic that the exploitation of an inexhaustible resource should ultimately fall victim to the technological advancements that swept the globe towards the end of the nineteenth century. Although inevitably damaged, the Turks & Caicos salt industry survived several hurricanes and even the economic slump created by the American Civil War. However, over the years, larger salt-producing areas such as Great Inagua and those in the Mediterranean were increasingly favoured over these smaller islands, as shipping costs could be reduced by operating larger vessels and only visiting a single port. By 1963 the salinas on Grand Turk, South Caicos and Salt Cay were for the large part abandoned, looking from a distance like muddy mosaics on a scrubby floor, their edges sparkling with brilliant white crystals, a poignant reminder of this once prized West Indian jewel.

The salt industry has now been inactive for well over three decades and the salinas are beginning to show signs of their industrial neglect. The metal sails of the more recent, wooden windmills stand idle, the briny breezes that used to spin them into life having long since rusted the iron cogs of the pumping mechanisms. Today they tower over the salt pan landscape, hallmarks of a bygone era. The once regular waterline has now surrendered to

Windmills still grace the skyline of the salt-producing islands, despite the industry having ended in the 1960s, though most of the metal vanes of the more modern designs have now all but rusted away in the salt-laden air. However, many of the walls, channels and sluice gates have remained in surprisingly good condition and some on Salt Cay have been fully restored to form a working museum, commemorating the historic salt industry of the Turks & Caicos Islands.

the advancing tide of salt-tolerant vegetation, such as the Buttonwood and herbaceous plants like Sea Purslane. Slowly, with the passage of time, the salinas are reverting back to their former verdant state. In places, the intricate stonework of the boundary walls has begun to crumble, with land crabs and lizards making the now undisturbed crevices their homes. With the relative lack of human activity, resident and migratory bird populations are now flourishing, as they take advantage of the teeming life that thrives in the shallow saline waters created by the redundant salt ponds. Of the rich avifauna that wade the brackish waters, herons, flamingos, stilts and sandpipers are in particular evidence. The diminutive Green Heron is commonly seen stalking along the water's edge, or amongst the mangrove pneumatophores in search of its piscine prey, while its larger cousin, the Reddish Egret, can be observed flamboyantly 'canopy feeding' in the centre of a salina.

Just as a beast of burden previously restrained by bridles and harnesses strides faster and more freely when released from its workload, the natural world also seems to rejoice in the liberation of the salinas. While the salt carts may be long gone, the donkeys still trek up and down the overgrown landscape, creating their own paths in a vista that time almost forgot.

Eking out an existence in the oxygen deficient sediments that border the salt ponds, a small sprig of Sea Purslane *(Salicornia sp.)* stands defiant in front of the watery expanse. Another salt-tolerant plant is the Buttonwood *(Conocarpus erectus)*, which occurs as green and silver-leaved varieties. Like mangroves, they often border the salinas and offer a resting place for birds such as the Brown Pelican *(Pelecanus occidentalis)* that fish in the still waters.

Life on a Thread

Whereas the Turks Islands had become occupied by Bermudian salt rakers as early as 1678, it took a series of world political events before the non salt-producing Caicos Islands became inhabited again, over one hundred years later. This sequence began when, following their defeat in the American War of Independence, thousands of Loyalists fled from the southern states of Georgia and the Carolinas to Florida, which had been in British hands since the end of the Seven Years War. Here they hoped to re-establish their lives by growing rice and tobacco, but their plans were thwarted when, only a few years later in 1783, they received some devastating news. At the Treaty of Paris, Florida had become repatriated to Spain and its English colonists had been given just eighteen months to settle their affairs and vacate the territory.

With no homes to return to in either Europe or America, many Loyalist planters looked to the nearby islands of the Bahamas, which Spain had relinquished to England as part of the same treaty. Upon application to London, they were granted large areas of unoccupied land to restart their plantations as a form of compensation for their previous losses. Records show that seventy-two Loyalists were granted over 18 000 acres of the uninhabited Caicos Islands, which at the time were encompassed under Bahamian legislation. Despite this, only forty families are believed to have eventually settled here, but they brought with them an estimated 1200 slaves. It is with a certain irony that an archipelago, robbed of its indigenous people by Spanish slavers and considered to hold little intrinsic value, was eventually to become largely recolonised by slaves, forcibly brought here to exploit the islands' natural resources that grew vigorously under the tropical sun.

For a short time the Loyalists prospered as they reaped the benefits bestowed by the virgin soil, choosing to cultivate primarily the Sea Island Cotton that was native to the region and for which demand back in England was soaring. As more plantations became established, it is likely that the islands underwent a rapid transformation from a motley array of shrubs, cacti and sprawling vines to fields of more uniform composition. This newly cultivated landscape would have changed with the

Yankee Town was first established on West Caicos in 1859 by a consortium of American merchants who intended to produce salt, but the American Civil War commenced only two years later and their venture failed. In 1890 the site was re-occupied for agricultural purposes and despite only a short tenure, both sisal and cotton can still be found on the island today, the ruins besieged by their now wild crops.

seasons, the green monotony being broken by an occasional dusting of white or purplish blossoms and fluffy white bolls of the tended cotton plants. Harvests were good and top prices were paid for this 'long staple' cotton, from which fine woven textiles could be produced for the British gentry. Of course, cheap labour was at the heart of the plantation's success, with an army of slaves continuously working the fields. While the task of removing the seeds from their valuable white hairs was soon to become mechanised with the introduction of the cotton gin, this paradoxically led to an increased demand for slaves who were now needed to prepare the greater quantities of cotton. Land prices soared and with Caicos cotton gaining rank among the best in the world, the Loyalist planters must have thought they could do no wrong in this, their newfound home.

All the unoccupied Caicos Islands eventually saw the establishment of cotton plantations, the boundaries of which were literally carved in stone. Encircling each property was a dry stone wall, fashioned out of local limestone rocks. Although these walls were probably erected more as a statement of ownership, they would have served as effective barriers to the

Sea Island Cotton *(Gossypium barbadense)* was present on the islands long before its cultivation in the Loyalist plantations. However, despite being a local species it was still susceptible to diseases and insect attack, especially when grown in large quantities. For farmers then and now, the delicate beauty of a resting butterfly, like the colourful Gulf Fritillary *(Agraulis vanillae)*, is always tainted by the destructive power of the caterpillars they produce.

Red Bugs *(Dysdercus sp.)* that once devastated the cotton plantations at the end of the eighteenth century are still present on the islands and can be seen here feeding on the sap of a local beach plant, known as Monkey Spoon *(Phyllanthus epiphyllanthus)*. These insects belong to a family of bugs that has the common name of 'Cotton Stainers', describing the damage they cause to the cotton fibres.

newly introduced domesticated grazers that may have otherwise roamed into the tended fields and trampled the valuable, fibrous crop. Blocks of the abundant soft limestone were also used to construct the plantation buildings, which generally comprised the main house, slave quarters and storage sheds. These were all painted brilliant white using a quicklime plaster produced from conch shells; an impressive testament to the resourcefulness of these new settlers. It may have taken some 250 years, but now a new community of Caicos settlers had been established, their one common trait being their loyalty to the British Crown.

Sadly, the Caicos cotton industry survived just thirty years, with the Great Hurricane of 1813 marking the dramatic end of its tempestuous history. Over this period the planters had witnessed both good and bad times, as they journeyed along a roller coaster of natural blessings and calamities. In 1789, their crop suffered from a heavy infestation of the Chenille Worm, an unfamiliar pest that they found impossible to control. Harvests of the fluffy bolls plummeted and when they eventually began to recover they were hit again, this time by a new pest, the Red Bug. This brightly coloured insect damages the developing bolls and transmits a fungus that discolours the cotton fibres, thereby reducing their value. However, both the cotton and the planters proved to be very resilient, and by the turn of the century cotton production from the Caicos plantations had exceeded the rest of the Bahamas. But, this voracious shrub eventually stripped the thin soil of its vital nutrients and minerals, leading to a gradual decline in productivity. For the few Loyalists who persevered with their plantations, the raging winds that devastated the islands in 1813 served as the final impetus to forsake their homes once again, this time having lost an arduous fight against Mother Nature.

More than one species of sisal exist within the islands, but the commercially important variety *(Agave sisalana)* was introduced around 1850. Another common name for the genus is the Century Plant, as it takes several years for their pole-like terminal flowering stage to appear, after which the parent plant dies. These tall structures are a common sight and often act as lookout posts for hunting birds like the American Kestrel *(Falco sparverius).*

Cheshire Hall plantation was established over 200 years ago and encompassed around 5000 acres of Providenciales, then known as Provident Cay, or Blue Caicos. Besides the outline of the main house, little is known about the site, except that it was named after the English home county of its owner, Thomas Stubbs. Failing to prosper, he eventually sold the land to his brother, Wade, who already owned a cotton plantation on North Caicos.

With failing crops behind them, many Loyalists chose to emigrate to Canada, Britain or other islands in the West Indies, though some moved just across the Columbus Passage to try their hand at salt raking. In their ignominious retreat, it was not only their homes the planters abandoned. Their slaves were also deserted, left to cope as best they could from subsistence farming and fishing. The liberated slaves, effectively freed twenty-one years before official emancipation, eventually congregated around Kew, North Caicos, where they established their own small-holdings within the plantation grounds. Uprooted from their native lands, these people were to make the Turks & Caicos their new home, their families becoming, in a twist of fate, the lasting pioneers and developers of these much fought-over cays.

Following the demise of the cotton industry, another crop in the form of sisal began to attract planters to the remote Caicos Islands. This succulent plant is an impressive looking agave species whose rosette of long, lance-like leaves yielded valuable coarse fibres that were once used for making rope. The dry, hot climate, already home to similar species, was considered to be ideally suited to growing the fibrous sisal and so large-scale cultivation commenced. Whereas North Caicos and Providenciales had supported the most successful cotton plantations, East and West Caicos were to become the main homes for the thriving sisal business that developed in the late nineteenth century. But, in the tradition of the boom and bust industries that have exploited these islands in the past, the production of sisal was to enjoy only a brief success, the harvest falling victim to both blight and competition from synthetic fibres.

Today the plantations are idle, their walls crumbling under years of neglect as they sink further into the ever-engulfing sea of vegetation. The buildings stand as mere shells, their wooden roofs having long since collapsed to be replaced by a living canopy of green frondescence. Free of human constraints, the cotton and sisal grow abundantly amidst a dense carpet of undergrowth, floral legacies of those yesteryears. Along with the history they represent, both plants are often overlooked, until the terminal flowering stage of the sisal thrusts aloft an imposing mast, which stands like a sentry watching over the land where crops were once king.

The Bountiful Sea

For a nation renowned for its undersea wonders, it is perhaps surprising that the Turks & Caicos support few commercial fisheries. That is until one delves into the underlying oceanography of this archipelago. The surrounding dark blue waters are far removed from the rich murky green of temperate seas, being virtually devoid of resident life. Even the famous Humpback Whales do not stop here, these mighty beasts being mere passers-by following an incredible migratory path. In fact, the nutrient-poor offshore waters have little to offer fishermen, yet have always served as their lifeline, bringing to the coasts the precious larvae upon which their livelihoods ultimately depend. Thus, the islanders have traditionally turned to the shallow waters for their seafood, where the expansive areas of white sand prevail.

Though the coral reefs may be teeming with fishes, the majority are both small and evasive, darting into crevices at the slightest hint of danger. Of course, there are larger predatory fish lurking about, and these make tasty rewards for the fishermen who have the patience and skill to catch them. But the reliance mainly on underwater marksmanship to capture these animals has meant that these reef fishes have fortunately escaped the heavy commercial exploitation that could quickly devastate their numbers. Understandably, slow-moving animals and those attached to the substratum are much easier to harvest, and historically this is where the local fisheries have focused.

One such industry that emerged in the late 1800s centred on the lowly sponge, an animal that is so inanimate it is often mistaken as a plant. These amazing creatures are mere bundles of loosely organised cells that survive by drawing in water through thousands of tiny pores covering their surfaces, stripping it of vital oxygen and food. This simple existence has allowed an extraordinary variety of shapes and sizes to be adopted; small encrusting mats, long slender tubes and gigantic barrels are but a few of the many growth forms that add to the surrealism of the tropical underwater landscape.

The fenestrate nature of the dried skeletons makes the husks very absorbent when removed from their fluid environment

Large Nassau Groupers *(Epinephelus striatus)* are often targeted by local fishermen, but within the Turks & Caicos they have, for the most part, been spared the commercial decimation found in many Caribbean nations. Other sizeable fish, like the iridescent Mahi-Mahi *(Coryphaena hippurus)*, come in from deep water to feed on the teaming Silversides, but their capture is more the goal of visiting anglers.

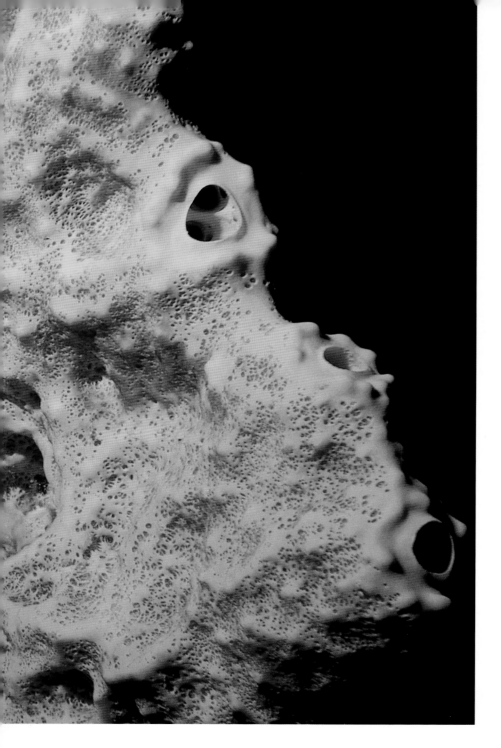

Sponges are a common
component of the reef
community and many
animals, like the Sponge Brittle
Star *(Ophiothrix suensonii)*, are found living on
and within their chambered bodies. When sponges
were commercially harvested, the price they would fetch
was based mainly on size, with the huge barrel varieties
being a prized commodity. However, their growth rates are
very slow and so the demise of the industry was perhaps
just a matter of time.

and therefore, it is little wonder that certain of these sessile animals became highly sought-after as household accessories. Spearheaded by the arrival of sponge divers from Greece, the Bahamas and Caicos Banks soon became a hive of activity for pioneering local fishermen, all eager to exploit the untapped riches of these waters. Often brightly pigmented, the native sponges proved easy to locate beneath the crystal clear waters of the Caicos Bank, and, being unable to move, they were just as easy to harvest. In fact, their collection was so simple that the fishermen could remain in their boats, bringing sponges aboard using an iron hook mounted on a long pole. By 1890, hundreds of sloops were operating within the Bahamas chain, making sponging an extremely important industry for these islands. As far as the Turks & Caicos were concerned, a new source of revenue had been added to their largely salt-based economy and one that far exceeded the funds generated by the trade in other marine resources.

With little concern for the environment at the turn of the century, the over-exploitation of this vulnerable group of creatures was sadly inevitable. As the natural stocks began to wane, efforts were made to sustain the high yields that had brought so much prosperity to the islands. The sponge's simplicity allowed for their artificial propagation using live 'clippings', which were cut from recently collected animals and fastened onto small cement blocks to weigh them down. Thousands upon thousands of cuttings were sown in the semi-enclosed waters of Bell Sound, South Caicos, and later in Chalk Sound, Providenciales, but this only served to rejuvenate the industry for a short while. Cheaper, synthetic substitutes began to flood the market and when a fungus hit the sponge banks in 1938 the fishery finally collapsed.

In stark contrast to the immobility of the sponge is the graceful agility of the turtle, a marine animal that is very much grounded in the cultural heritage of the Turks & Caicos. Although with their nimble manoeuvres these reptiles are capable of evading the

Although no longer collected in the islands, sponges have always had natural predators. Queen Angelfish *(Holacanthus ciliaris)* feed almost exclusively on them and one can be seen here tucking into its favourite diet. As a result, many sponges have toxins and tough outer skins but, even so, few are able to deter the advances of a Hawksbill Turtle *(Eretmochelys imbricata)*, which will often take a single bite before moving on, providing a poignant lesson in resource management.

Hawksbill Turtles *(Eretmochelys imbricata)* are built to an ancient design, with their armour plating and surprising underwater agility serving the species well over the millennia. More recently the attractive overlapping plates that form their shell have led to their world-wide decline, as their numbers have been decimated, mainly in the Indo-Pacific, to supply the 'tortoise-shell' jewellery trade.

most awesome of underwater predators, they must always return to the surface to breathe, where they can often be seen bobbing around like large pieces of flotsam basking in the warmth of the tropical sun. Here, with their heads in the air and eyesight attuned to the aquatic realm, an unwary individual can leave itself open to attack from both above and below.

Turtles have been hunted for their meat since the days of the Taino Indians, when the seas are believed to have supported much greater numbers, as suggested by the large quantities of turtle bones retrieved from archaeological sites. Centuries of over-harvesting, however, have caused a substantial decrease in their numbers throughout the world. Despite this, the local population appears sound and probably remains one of the healthiest in the Greater Caribbean. All species of marine turtles currently enjoy legal protection against any international trade, though the islanders are still able to fish this traditional seafood for home consumption. The most sizeable species landed are the Loggerhead and Green Turtles, which can provide enough food for the largest of families. So saying, big turtles are rarely caught and further regulations prevent the harvest of gravid females that have hauled themselves onto a sandy beach to nest. In addition, it is illegal to collect turtle eggs because, with only one in approximately ten thousand hatchlings surviving through to adulthood, the odds are already stacked against these ancient creatures.

Cautiously peering from beneath their protective shell, the stalked eyes of a Queen Conch *(Strombus gigas)* check the surrounding seascape for unwelcome visitors, before the animal continues to feed on algae growing amongst the seagrass. Adult conch often bury themselves in the sand, leaving only the upper surfaces of their shells exposed, which often leads to clumps of Fuzzy Finger Algae *(Dasycladus* sp.*)* adorning their tops like a head of unkempt hair.

Ever since humans have lived in the Turks & Caicos, the Queen Conch has been a continual source of nourishment, serving the needs of the Tainos, the slaves and now today's islanders, as well as the export market to America. This marine creature begins its life circulating in the plankton, but after a few weeks and

A local islander demonstrates how to 'knock' a conch. This involves making a small hole in the third spiral of the shell and then using a knife to cut the adductor muscle, the only solid attachment the animal has to its portable abode. Its slimy body contains a reputedly fine aphrodisiac, the straw-like crystalline style, which is part of the digestive system, but it is the large, leathery muscular foot that the animal uses to drag itself across the sand that forms the highly prized meat.

possibly several hundred miles from its hatching site, it settles in the shallow waters to grow. Following their larval wanderings, the young conch are thought to remain hidden in the soft sandy sediments for one to two years, only venturing above the surface when their bluntly spiked shell has attained sufficient thickness to afford moderate protection against more agile and speedy predators.

With age, the Queen Conch eventually becomes invulnerable to the crushing power of even the most formidable jaws, but this strength provides little protection against human ingenuity. It was discovered that by simply using the spire of another conch, a round hole could be 'knocked' in the shell, detaching the animal from its home. Carbon dating of 'fossilised' shells has revealed that this technique has in fact been adopted for several hundred years. Today, small steel hammers held in experienced hands make light work of this task, leaving behind seemingly undamaged shells marked only by the human calling card of a narrow slit. Traditionally, small fishing boats were towed by locally made sailing sloops to the rich conching grounds, where their quarries were sighted using glass-bottomed buckets. A two-pronged conch hook was then worked under the shell and the animal brought to the surface by raising the long wooden pole hand over hand. But gradually, canvas sails gave way to speedy outboard engines and today virtually all conch are collected using fast motor boats that are required to access the more remote areas of the banks. The conch hook has also been replaced by the grasping hands of the modern free diver, who is able, with experience, to collect up to seven conch on a single breath, often in waters of appreciable depth.

The ornately whorled shell, with its lustrous rosy-pink lining, has also found various applications over the years, from carving tools used by the Tainos to quicklime for the Loyalist homes. Not surprisingly, the conch's beautiful shell has also had historical appeal as an ornament, though no commercial exploitation occurred until the late 1950s when a shell industry was established on South Caicos to supply Florida with fanciful marine curios. For a short time, the shell commanded a higher price than the meat and the conch needed to be processed in a different manner, hanging the snail by its muscular foot until the sheer weight of the shell pulled the animal out of its protective home. Although there is still some demand for conch shells for decorative purposes, for the most part the market has primarily focused on the meat, prompting fishermen to discard the heavy shells on the shallow banks to lighten their boats for the homeward journey. On popular conching grounds, huge piles of knocked shells have subsequently accumulated, forming expansive areas of hard substratum on an otherwise sandy seafloor. Here, on these artificial reefs, new communities flourish with juvenile reef fish, octopus and lobsters all seeking safe refuge amongst the many crevices freshly created within these conch 'middens'.

The shells that have been discarded on land also make for an imposing sight, in places transforming the low-lying cactus landscape to one of new height. Middleton Cay, once home to much Taino trading activity, boasts many impressive middens, some attaining over ten feet in height. These knocked shells all

The large size and beautiful pink lining of Queen Conch shells *(Strombus gigas)* have an obvious ornamental value and are often used in the islands as a decorative trim for the top of a wall. Other conchs occur locally, but are not harvested for food and are therefore rarely seen. The creamy coloured shell of the Milk Conch *(Strombus costatus)* is smaller but much thicker, which simply represents more effort for less reward.

Knocked conch shells lie in huge piles at the southern end of Middleton Cay, South Caicos. Although this is a common sight on other Caribbean islands, it is relatively unusual for the Turks & Caicos, for the fishermen generally knock the conch at sea and discard the shells overboard. As well as helping with fuel costs, this local practice provides much appreciated dwellings for small fish, like this juvenile Longfin Damselfish *(Stegastes diencaeus)*.

bear the narrow-slits of modern times and are therefore believed to be relatively new additions to this historic cay, the vivid pink and orange hues of the most recent arrivals contrasting sharply with the brilliant whiteness of the bleached shells beneath. Look a little lower, though, and black and grey shells can be seen embedded in the underlying rock, fossilised in the calcareous beach sediments that have been sun-baked and weathered to form a cement-like deposit. Continued erosion by the gentle lapping waves has revealed the internal spiral intricacies of these shells, the former residents of which probably last crawled across the bank some 500 years ago.

Whereas conch have much historical value, the other main export fishery of the Turks & Caicos has only gained importance over the last few decades. During this period the international reputation of lobster as seafood has escalated and today the Caribbean Spiny Lobster is considered by many to epitomise gourmet cuisine. While the waters surrounding the Turks & Caicos are a particular stronghold for this spiny invertebrate, to appreciate their presence we really have to pay a visit to the reef at night. When the sun has set, these wary arthropods seem to emerge from nowhere to forage for food, their five pairs of legs scuttling across both coral and sand in an amazingly co-ordinated fashion. During the day, these crustaceans aggregate in suitable holes and crevices in the reef, sometimes with several hundred individuals squeezing into the same small refuge. Presumably there is safety in numbers, as an occupied den is seemingly always more attractive to a stray lobster than an empty one. Also, the larger animals tend to stand guard over the smaller, thrashing their thorned antennae outside the entrance like épées in a fencing duel. However, the threat of a real intruder usually elicits an ungainly backwards scuttle into their comfort zone rather than a brave lunge forward in the form of a lobster attack.

The spiny defences of this crustacean have also presented an interesting challenge to fishermen over the years and have

Caribbean Spiny Lobsters *(Panulirus argus)* spend their days hidden in crevices, waiting for the cover of darkness before venturing out to feed. Only upon close inspection is it possible to determine the sex of these animals, with the females having a small 'thumb' on the last pair of her walking legs. This structure is used to tend her eggs, which appear as an orange mass on the underside of her tail and which remain there until the tiny larvae hatch.

ultimately been responsible for the Turks & Caicos now being able to boast some of the best free divers in the world. Although these days virtually all lobsters are hooked from their dens by fishermen wearing mask and fins, this technique has only been popular since the late 1970s when it replaced the inefficient snare that was being used at the time. The traditional means of lobstering, however, is with a 'bully-net', dipped over the side of a small boat. After locating an occupied den with a water glass, the animals were poked out with the aid of a 'tickler'. Once in the open, they were swept off the bottom using the scoop-like net. Although some islanders still practise bully-netting for subsistence purposes, this technique is not viable for the commercial fishery as many of the shallow water grounds have already been overfished. In spite of its elaborate armature and elusive nature, the lobster's only real defence to intense fishing pressure is to remain in depths beyond the reach of man. But, with the incredible breath-hold dives of some fishermen attaining depths in excess of one hundred feet, their sanctuaries have to be very deep indeed.

Today, in an effort to protect these important marine resources from over-exploitation, the conch and lobster fisheries are subject to strict regulations, such as size restrictions, a closed season and maximum quotas. Partially offset by their increased revenue, the landings of these animals nevertheless appear to be diminishing each year, making it increasingly difficult for the fishermen to make a living. Still of great social and economic significance, particularly to the islanders of South Caicos, the overall contribution of the fisheries to the Turks & Caicos economy has for some time been outstripped by the revenue created by the tourist trade. Consequently, the splendid marine life that surrounds these islands is now being viewed in a different light, with the 'Big Grab' of the first few days of the lobster season gradually succumbing in importance to the year-round influx of visitors who come to bask in the natural beauty of these islands.

Here, free divers take a few breaths of air before returning below the waves. Within the islands, lobsters are almost solely collected through breath-hold diving and are removed from their dens using a long hook. Good fishermen not only have the stamina to spend all day swimming down to great depths, they invariably return to the surface clutching three or more lobsters.

CHAPTER FOUR

New Horizons

A Cornucopia of Delights

A beautiful curtain of ivory sand lies draped upon the borders of a limestone island, the individual grains tumbling up and down the beach as if rejoicing in the gentle caress of the crystal clear Atlantic waters. A small flock of birds works the shore in search of the morning's offerings, as a school of tiny fish jump in perfect synchrony from the sea, creating silvery arcs like shimmering rainbows as they attempt to evade a threat concealed below the waves. Offshore dolphins revel in the freedom of the open ocean, while inland, just past the high strandline, the feathery plumes of Sea Oats sway in a warm breeze and small lizards scurry among the undergrowth. With the Turks & Caicos beaches being ranked as some of the best in the world, this description could apply to most that fringe this small archipelago. What may be surprising to learn is that a perfect likeness can be found along the picturesque twelve mile sandy stretch of Grace Bay on Providenciales, behind which lies the nation's main area of coastal development.

During the 'Golden Age of Piracy' (1690-1720), Providenciales and its associated cays acted as a refuge for some of the most infamous buccaneers that plundered the Greater Caribbean. Calico Jack used these strategic islands as his hideaway after fleeing the former pirate capital of Nassau, which had succumbed to an unwelcome peace imposed by British warships. With a crew of cut-throats that included the two female pirates, Mary Read and Anne Bonny, this flamboyant character frequently returned here and beached his ship on its side, careening the vessel in an effort to disguise its shape from any passing patrols. Often oblivious to this significant piece of local history, a new type of visitor now seeks sanctuary within these secluded islands. Each year thousands of tourists come to enjoy the cornucopia of delights that Providenciales has to offer, to soak up the sun and to relax in a world of splendid natural vistas.

Up until the mid 1960s, Providenciales, or 'Provo', had only three small settlements that were linked by simple donkey tracks cut through the undergrowth. The Cheshire Hall cotton plantation had long since been abandoned and the few hundred islanders enjoyed uncomplicated lives that relied upon subsistence fishing and farming. But all this was about to change when in 1966 a group of investors visited the island and immediately recognised

Previously a haven for pirates, who would return to these shores to hide with their ill-gotten gains, the beautiful beaches of Providenciales are now playing host to an ever-increasing number of discerning tourists. Even though most of the recent development has concentrated along the shores of Grace Bay, this seemingly endless stretch of white sand still offers seclusion for those who seek it.

its potential as a tourist destination. Welcoming an opportunity that promised economic prosperity, the local and British governments granted these pioneering developers 4000 acres of coastal land under a lease-purchase agreement. Within just a few years the villages of Blue Hills, Five Cays and The Bight became connected for the first time by road and the newly constructed airstrip put the pleasures of Provo within just ninety minutes of Miami. As the wheels of progress turned, the island was gradually transformed into the paradise retreat that we know today. Where it differs from most other Caribbean islands, however, is in being able to offer first class facilities while at the same time retaining the simple character of its former years. Having learned from the mistakes of other nations, the Turks & Caicos adopted a very cautious approach to their tourism development and thankfully these restraints are reflected in the beautiful low-level West Indian architecture and tropical landscaped gardens that are key to the island's appeal.

With employment opportunities now widespread, many Turks Islanders returned to their homeland from the Bahamas and elsewhere, causing the local community to swell and rejuvenating

Despite the exceedingly low rainfall, the gardens that surround the resorts and hotels of the Turks & Caicos bloom with vibrant colours and lush tropical greenery. Careful tending and efficient irrigation ensure that palm trees, bromeliads and hibiscus thrive alongside the more delicate varieties of ferns, orchids and lilies.

the sense of national pride among its people. Today the population comprises the native Turks Islanders and naturalised 'belongers', who have left their own countries, in particular Jamaica, Haiti, Canada, America and England, to make these 'Islands of June' their new home. Though the year long pleasant climate undoubtedly helps and the idyllic surroundings cannot fail but create a tranquil atmosphere, it is the warmth and generosity of the local people that make visitors feel as if they are welcome guests in some Caribbean Shangri-La. Indeed, it is difficult to know whether the Tourist Board's slogan, 'Beautiful by Nature', was meant to refer to the exquisite natural artistry of the islands, or to the genuine friendliness of its people.

Over the last three decades internationally acclaimed hotels, wonderful marinas, fine à la carte restaurants, water-sports galore and even a casino have arrived in Provo, yet much of the land remains undeveloped, protected from the bulldozer's onslaught by the government's National Park system. In 1992, more than thirty sanctuaries, reserves, parks and historical sites were designated throughout the islands in an effort to conserve and manage the bountiful natural resources on offer. Nonetheless, the vegetation

Visitors to these islands are guaranteed to meet friendly faces wherever they go. The local people are certainly blessed with a cheerful outlook on life and you will often hear the phrase 'It's all good!' Other than relaxation on idyllic secluded beaches, the activities available for tourists are mainly geared towards water-sports and, with a strong cultural background in fisheries, many boats are available to take you out for a day's adventure.

on Provo is slowly being transformed as the seeds of introduced plants gradually become established among the native flora, adding new colour to the untamed landscape. From the air, one area of north-east Provo looks especially different, appearing as a luxuriant expanse amidst the sun-baked shrubby terrain. Mirror-like ponds reflect the powder blue sky as they chronicle the passage of the fluffy white clouds that slowly drift above the island, blown by the cooling trade winds. The land, fitted with an emerald carpet, is more reminiscent of Tennyson's English countryside than the tropical Turks & Caicos, the perfectly manicured lawns bursting with vitality under the midday sun. This aberration in the landscape is not a mirage, but the spectacular result of man satiating nature's thirst. Each day up to 300 000 gallons of desalinated water are pumped onto this 200 acre site via an extensive underground irrigation system, transforming the semi-arid vegetation into a lush verdant oasis. Receiving on average only twenty inches of rain each year, Provo may seem an unlikely destination to support a championship eighteen hole golf course. However, one was built here in 1992 that has since gained the accolade of being among the best conditioned in the whole of the Greater Caribbean.

Wildlife abounds on both the greens and fairways of the Provo Golf Course, with this young Curly Tail Lizard *(Leiocephalus sp.)* warming itself on a convenient rock adjacent to the fourteenth hole. But, for those times when nature can become a pest, the numerous water hazards are kept well stocked with the aptly named Mosquito Fish *(Gambusia affinis)*, which can consume its own weight in mosquito larvae on a daily basis.

Designed around the natural features of the area, the seventy-two par course encompasses over twelve acres of landscaped ponds, which not only make for challenging play, but also attract a magnificent array of avian spectators to the region. When teeing off from the forth hole it is not uncommon to be watched by a small flock of Greater Flamingos that come to feed in the adjacent lake, their pink coloration as vibrant against the turf-covered backdrop as the flags that mark the player's goal. Ducks too seem unperturbed by the sporting activity and the colourful Ground Doves are never too far away, ready to take advantage of any seeds that may have been unearthed by the golfers' shoes.

Far from destroying precious habitat, the Provo Golf Course has added greatly to the local environment, becoming a haven for wildlife and visiting birds, including the rare migrant Kirkland's Warbler. The 4000 palm trees, intended to act as safety buffers against any stray shots, have become home to a chorus of birds that provide background music with their melodious song. Indigenous vegetation, flourishing under the irrigation, is complemented by introduced flowering plants, such as Bougainvillaea and Hibiscus, which decorate the borders of the fairways and greens with welcome bursts of bright colours. Hummingbirds flit from blossom to blossom where they hover like fairies, using their long slender tongues to feed upon the plentiful nectar. On the ground, Curly Tail Lizards can be seen scampering across the trimmed grass, occasionally stopping with their heads poised high, as if to admire their beautiful home.

Like the golf course, many of Provo's attractions revolve around the natural splendours of the islands and sports fishing is no exception. While the clear offshore waters of the Turks & Caicos may lack the rich planktonic life of temperate seas, they are home to a surprising number of large pelagic species that each year attract hundreds of sports fishing enthusiasts. The top predatory fishes they seek all have torpedo-shaped bodies and deeply forked tails, making them very agile and capable of extremely impressive speeds that challenge the ability of even the

Slowly striding past a backdrop of blazing bougainvillaea a rather stately Great Egret *(Egretta alba)* hunts for prey, its pure white plumage an impressive sight. Even for a heron, this bird has an exceptionally long slender neck, the bend in the middle allowing it to be folded back on itself. A winter visitor to the Turks & Caicos, the Great Egret can be easily distinguished from the resident Cattle Egret *(Bubulcus ibis)* by its larger size.

most skillful angler. During the cooler months, fishers may battle against a mighty Bluefin Tuna or the beautiful, but strangely shaped, Mahi-Mahi, both of which rip the line from the reel as they struggle in their fight for freedom. In the summer, however, the giant Blue Marlin steals the show as individuals, which often exceed ten feet in length, migrate through the local waters. These magnificent creatures are certainly built for speed, their long sinuous bodies representing a supercharged engine of muscle-powered propulsion, streamlined from nose to tail, with even their dorsal fins folding back into a special groove to reduce drag. Using huge eyes to hunt ocean-going fish and squid, they debilitate their mobile prey with a swipe from their hefty bills, before swallowing it whole through a mouth that bears no teeth. Because of their lightning attacks, special techniques have to be employed to entice these monsters from the deep to become snared on an angler's hook. Vessels are equipped with outriggers that hold the line at the best angle, causing the lures to 'pop and fizz', making short hops out of the sea while leaving long bubble trails behind them. If a marlin strikes the bait, the line is pulled from the outrigger causing the lure to slow in the water, as if stunned, and giving time for the fish to engulf its booby-trapped prize. Once hooked the tremendous power of this animal is brought into

Hanging from the wooden gallows of the Turtle Cove marina, a 300 lb Blue Marlin *(Makaira nigricans)* seems to watch the awe-struck passers-by. The dark colour of its skin, however, reveals its demise, for when alive these fish are a metallic blue, with white bars that stripe their flanks. It is uncertain as to why they lose their bright markings, but perhaps they are merely saving their true beauty for the freedom of the ocean realm.

Powerful engines churn the water into a frenzy of foam as the marlin boats return to port just ahead of a sudden rainsquall. While under way, the long outriggers are held close to the sides, but when fishing they reach out at right angles, spreading the lines for best effect. Also, the precarious 'flying bridge' allows the skipper to navigate from on high, providing the best vantage point to spot reefs and schooling fish.

stark reality as the line screams from the reel. The fish often dances across the surface of the water, leaping and pirouetting in a spellbinding display, which is actually an attempt to use its tail to dislodge the lure from its mouth. Failing this, the fish plunges down into the abyssal depths, dragging out hundreds of yards of line and thus commencing the battle 'twixt man and beast.

Around this time of year, prestigious billfish tournaments are held in the Turks & Caicos and the marinas are gradually transformed into showpieces of marine engineering, as the elite marlin boats dominate the berths. Recognising the need for conservation, most marlin anglers are keen to observe a 'catch and release' protocol, and the competitions have strict rules to ensure that only the largest specimens are ever brought onto the back decks of the boats. The vast majority of the fish reeled in never leave the ocean and, once the lure has been removed, a deck hand will often tow a fatigued marlin by holding its bill, flushing water over its gills to revive the animal before its release. Also, many anglers voluntarily mark fish with special tags in an attempt to aid research into the lifecycle of marlins and help ensure the survival of one of the world's largest bony fishes for future generations.

As night draws in over the Turtle Cove marina, the muted tones of the setting sun are reflected in the gleaming white hulls of the now idle marlin boats. During a tournament, the crews are up well before dawn, readying their vessels and preparing the numerous rods and lures for the day ahead. They navigate out past the reef to await the starter's signal. Then, with a roar of engines, the fleet lifts from the water and each boat thunders off to its preferred location.

Besides deep sea fishing, the Turks & Caicos also offer near unrivalled opportunities to fish the famed Bonefish that feed over the shallow sandy banks on each incoming tide. With their silvery flanks reflecting the dappled sunlight as it skips over the sand ripples, these fish are remarkably elusive creatures, their presence being revealed only by the 'muds' of disturbed water they create as they forage for buried invertebrates. Despite being much smaller than their pelagic relatives, Bonefish can take off at speeds exceeding forty miles per hour, making them, pound for pound, the king of all swimmers. It is this furious fight once hooked that attracts the anglers' attention and although many may be caught by avid enthusiasts, most consider these fish too bony to eat and very few are removed from the marine environment. The satisfaction of beating such an unrelenting opponent is usually prize enough and releasing them is an excellent way to conserve yet another natural resource of these islands.

The shallow turquoise waters of Chalk Sound are an angler's delight, being a favoured haunt of the much-prized Bonefish *(Albula vulpes)*. Like the marlin, these fish have stiff, deeply forked tails, which allow them to accelerate rapidly and attain incredible underwater speeds. Bonefish also have special eyelids that act like swimming goggles, affording them excellent vision even in low visibility.

Aquatic Adventures

With the Turks & Caicos being fringed with over 200 miles of coral reefs, it is little wonder that a large proportion of visitors arrive ready to scuba dive, or are tempted to embark on their first aquatic adventures during their stay. However, unlike many Caribbean destinations, there are three characteristics of the local waters that are guaranteed to captivate novices and surprise even the most experienced divers. These are the amazing clarity of the coastal seas, the breathtaking reef drop-offs and the unerring frequency of encounters with charismatic marine life. In general, the underwater visibility remains around 80–100 feet, but, when the conditions are right, a diver's field of view can often exceed an astounding 200 feet. This exceptional water clarity can be explained by a combination of the islands' geography, geology and biology. Being miles from any major landmasses and situated in nutrient-poor oceanic waters, there are no nearby rivers offloading their cargoes of sediment and little plankton is present to cloud the seas. Around the coasts, the underwater movement of the fine sand is kept in check by the abundant seagrass beds and when the rains eventually do fall on land, the water merely seeps down through the porous limestone bedrock.

But crystal clear waters are of little importance if there is nothing to see and, in this respect, the Turks & Caicos rarely disappoint.

Even the topography of the reefs can capture the imagination, with intricately sculpted mountains of coral rising and falling in spellbinding undulations that finally plummet down sheer walls to depths of over 7000 feet. Few types of dive can beat the sheer exhilaration of effortlessly hovering along the walls of such abyssal cliffs, their colossal majesty unfolding before a group of dwarfed divers. As if this backdrop was not enough, some of the more impressive denizens of the deep regularly swim by, casting a nonchalant eye towards those curious humans that fizz with bubbles like effervescent tablets. Hawksbill, Green and Loggerhead Turtles are common passers-by, along with Southern Stingrays, Nurse Sharks, Reef Sharks and the always elegant Spotted Eagle Rays. Occasionally, Bottlenose and Atlantic Spotted Dolphins grace divers with their presence, while, at the right time of the year, it is possible to see the awesome Manta Rays and Humpback Whales gliding past the drop-offs.

Swimmers make their way ashore to West Caicos during their interval between dives. Some of the best wall diving can be had adjacent to this island and many of the dive operators from Providenciales regularly make the twenty mile journey to dive the numerous moored sites. Here it is possible to see Manta Rays *(Manta birostris)* filter feeding on plankton as they swim close to the reef.

The phenomenal local diving has been recognised since the 1960s, when South Caicos operated what was reputed to be among the first dive-orientated hotels in the Caribbean. It would seem, though, that for many years the clientele were able to keep their underwater exploits a closely guarded secret, as it is only recently that this small tropical nation has become a diving Mecca. With the vast majority of visitors spending their time on Provo, diving opportunities for most are generally restricted to the adjacent bays, West Caicos and a few of the nearby cays. For the uninitiated, it may be assumed that with the islands being so close together, a dive off one island will be much the same as any other. However, the reefs do not form a uniform coralline seascape and the submerged part of each island is like the terra firma above, having its own unique character despite a common ancestry.

For Provo, the north-facing reefs along Grace Bay are renowned for their defined spur and groove formations, with buttresses of coral jutting out like craggy fingers, alternating with brilliant white sand chutes. These relatively shallow dive sites with inshore mini-walls contrast markedly with the dramatic drop-offs and

Most of the local dive sites incorporate some aspect of wall diving, either mini-walls that descend to around fifty feet, or the true drop-offs that plummet to the ocean floor thousands of feet below. Having explored a small section of a wall, a group of divers ascends over the reef crest and makes its way back across sandy slopes to a waiting boat. Visibility often exceeds 100 feet, but it is always wise to dive new sites with a guide as you can easily become disorientated.

Little Water Cay,
with its population of endemic
Rock Iguanas, lies within one of the thirty-three protected
areas scattered throughout the island group. These
comprise National Parks, Sanctuaries, Nature Reserves and
Historical Sites that not only cover the land, but also
include the surrounding seas in an effort to safeguard the
delicate ecosystems for future generations.

Princess Alexandra Land and Sea National Park encompasses the whole of Grace Bay, Providenciales, where most of the major tourist development has occurred. The protected area extends from the white sandy beach all the way out to the deep water drop-off. Signs that outline the regulations have been placed at most of the access points and dive operators using the moored sites along the fringing reef remind visitors they are about to enter a marine park.

swim-throughs found at North West Point and those along the leeward side of West Caicos. Across the dividing Columbus Passage the coral gardens of Grand Turk and Salt Cay are a delight to behold. Being sheltered from the prevailing easterlies, a magnificent exhibition of living architecture has formed, with finely branched corals growing in such profusion they crowd together within easy reach of the shore. On the opposite coastlines of East and South Caicos, the same trade winds often cause a succession of white-capped breakers to buffet the shores. Here, the reefs are mainly formed by hardy species, the more delicate ones only being found below the influence of the Atlantic rollers. Sea fans flex in tune to the rhythmic water movements, benefiting from the food supply brought to them by the strong currents, while small fish struggle to maintain a refuge out of sight of the patrolling predators. Although the coral cover may be relatively low, the undersea walls of South Caicos and Long Cay are undoubtedly the best place to see species of marine megafauna. Thirty-strong schools of Eagle Rays, large Hammerheads, Whalesharks, resident pods of Dolphins and breeding aggregations of Nurse Sharks are not uncommon sightings. It is almost a certainty that the little explored reefs of East, Middle and North Caicos hold similar wonders that are just waiting to be discovered by the intrepid diver.

To their credit, the people of the Turks & Caicos were quick to realise the importance of the unique reefs that surround their homeland and took early steps to protect their valuable coastal resources. By establishing numerous marine parks, reserves and sanctuaries throughout the archipelago, the activities within their boundaries have been limited, helping to preserve the delicate balance of the local ecosystems. Under the slogan 'Take only pictures, leave only bubbles', it is now illegal to remove anything, live or dead, from the National Parks, with fishing and hunting being strictly regulated. Over time, the natural attractions of the popular dive sites have remained intact, a commendable achievement that would be impossible without the help of the environmentally conscious dive operators. Many of the parks appear to function as a magnet, drawing in both people and marine life, with unperturbed reef fish boldly confronting bemused divers in a manner seldom seen elsewhere in the Greater Caribbean.

For the sake of the reef it is a good policy to stay well clear of the fragile corals, but, if you forget, colonies of fire coral are there to remind you, their tiny hair-like tentacles packing a powerful sting if touched. The growth form of the Branching Fire Coral *(Millepora alcicornis)* easily distinguishes it from the other locally abundant species, Blade Fire Coral *(Millepora complanata)*, which is seen here with a pair of Blue Tangs *(Acanthurus coeruleus)*.

Dispersed throughout the marine protected areas are fixed buoys, which have been deployed at the most popular dive sites. These allow access to the reefs, but at the same time limit human impact, ensuring that the boats in which the divers arrive can be moored without using an anchor, a practice which can be very harmful to the corals. While anchoring is allowed in large sand patches, heavy fines can be levied against anyone who causes

physical damage to the reef. But, although the government and dive operators both play an important role in reef protection, each visitor to the islands must also assume responsibility for ensuring the Turks & Caicos remain pristine. Most divers will agree that buoyancy control is the key to enjoyable diving, but this skill also makes sense when considering the health of the reef. Growing only a fraction of an inch each year, coral branches representing decades of effort can be destroyed in seconds by the careless kick of a diver. So, until complete awareness of one's equipment and body posture has been achieved, keeping a respectful distance is probably the best policy. But in the case of a memory lapse, the powerful sting of the abundant 'fire coral' reminds us to stay clear, these species acting as effective on-site enforcers of approved reef etiquette.

Besides the spectacular marine life, the favourable chance of finding historic ship wrecks has also attracted much diver attention, even though any discoveries by unlicensed questers remain the property of the government under British common law. Nonetheless, the last few decades have seen treasure hunters from across the globe visit these remote islands in search of Spanish gold or priceless artefacts, but much of the local waters still remain unexplored. In 1978, treasure worth millions of

Encrusted with corals and algae, a centuries-old anchor lies embedded in the reef at White Face, West Caicos. Many divers swim past this camouflaged piece of history, not recognising its shape or realising its significance. Similarly, the reefs' smaller inhabitants are often overlooked and a keen eye can sometimes spot the Yellowhead Jawfish *(Opistognathus aurifrons)*, the males of which use their mouths to incubate the eggs.

Often the true colours of a reef are best seen at shallow
snorkelling sites, where the light is at its strongest. Foureye
Butterflyfish *(Chaetodon capistratus)* are conspicuous
residents here and are usually seen in breeding pairs, which
are believed to remain together for life. These fish feed on
coral polyps and, when their populations are high, as in the
local waters, it is thought to indicate a healthy reef.

dollars was discovered on the nearby Silver Shoals and, only two years later, another company located the remains of an early sixteenth century ship near Molasses Reef on the Caicos Bank. Although historians were disappointed to learn that the latter was not the one lost by Columbus on his maiden voyage, this wreck remains the oldest European ship discovered in the Americas. Its watery grave has since been protected as an historic site, while the vast majority of artefacts can be viewed without even getting wet, as they now form an impressive display in the National Museum on Grand Turk.

Many remnants of the tall ships that once frequented these waters are scattered across the reefs, but the rich encrusting growth can often disguise even the most recognisable structures. Once pointed out, however, the anchors and cannons of yesteryear begin to take shape amidst the living substratum and a new type of magic is unveiled on the reefs of the Turks & Caicos. A few marine historic sites can be explored by snorkel, such as the cannons off Fort George Cay, just a short boat ride east of Provo. In addition, the National Museum has created an archaeological snorkel trail on Grand Turk that allows visitors to follow an underwater path littered with ancient cannons, anchors and other artefacts discovered on the nearby reefs. For the non-diver, much of the marine splendours of these islands can be viewed by simply snorkelling off a beach onto a small patch reef. With this aim in mind, snorkel trails have been established at the

Now known throughout the world, Jo Jo the wild Bottlenose Dolphin is pictured here with his own warden, Dean Bernal. When not checking on Jo Jo's welfare, Dean works with the Jo Jo Dolphin Project, which looks after this special individual and aims to protect other local cetaceans along with their precious marine home.

most popular locations, notably on Smith's Reef and White House Reef off Provo and Admiral's Aquarium Reef off South Caicos. In spite of the shallow depths, there is still much to see: Queen, Princess and Stoplight Parrotfishes bite at the algae-covered limestone, Blue Tangs and French Grunts congregate in great schools and Hawksbill Turtles take refuge under rocky outcrops. Few of the reef species are absent from these sites and, with their ease of access and good lighting, they offer some of the best photographic opportunities for amateur and professionals alike.

Capturing a snap shot of a dolphin would certainly be an achievement and, for many, the chance to swim with one may represent a life-long ambition. But, in the calm water of Grace Bay this dream can often become reality because, ever since 1980, a wild Bottlenose Dolphin has been interacting with humans under his own volition. Although 'Jo Jo' is known to swim with other dolphins, he seems to prefer human companionship and regularly escorts sail and dive boats, either riding the bow waves or playing in the wake. His untiring

fascination with humans and their activities has unfortunately led to repeated accidents, with Jo Jo having been injured several times by propellers, fishing line and the like. Having attained the status of a local celebrity, pressure was eventually brought to bear and, in 1989, Jo Jo was officially appointed a warden for protection. Since then, the Jo Jo Dolphin Project has developed, working not only to safeguard this exceptional dolphin, but also other marine mammals and the environment in which they live. Educating locals and visitors is also given high priority, as although swimming with Jo Jo can be a life-changing experience, it must always be remembered that he is a wild animal and if threatened he will defend himself.

Few experiences can surpass the pure elation of playing with a dolphin in its natural habitat, though witnessing a Humpback Whale escort her new-born calf through clear sunlit waters must surely be one. Positioned just sixty miles north-west of the world's largest Humpback breeding ground, the Turks & Caicos have gained the enviable reputation of providing divers with some of the best chances of encountering these underwater leviathans. Migrating from as far north as the Gulf of Maine, Newfoundland and Greenland, each winter thousands of these gentle giants leave their summer feeding grounds and head south for their winter sojourn in the West Indies. Following the contours of the deep Atlantic trenches, many pass straight through the Columbus Passage, coming very close to either South Caicos or Grand Turk.

From December to February, the waters echo with the haunting song of the males, their long moans being audible for many miles. Divers can hear not only these soulful laments, but also feel the sound waves vibrate within their rib cages as the males call to attract a mate. Usually sighted off the wall, these magnificent animals occasionally wander over the reef crest, where their grey bulk acts like a solitary cloud casting a huge shadow over the kaleidoscope of activity beneath. But it is only over deeper water where they engage in their amazing acrobatic displays that have helped to convert our interest in them from that of a valuable commodity to one of inspiring beauty worthy of protection. Sometimes hurling their whole bodies out of the water as they breach, these forty ton animals seem to rejoice in the warm waters of the tropics, the scale of their visual and acoustic displays being unrivalled within the animal kingdom. Upon diving, their uniquely patterned tail flukes slowly rise into the air, revealing these individuals to be regular visitors to the Turks & Caicos. And with continued protection, it is to be hoped that the offspring of their own calves will embark on the same incredible journey, gracing these shores for many years to come.

Humpback Whales *(Megaptera novaeangliae)* use the deep-water passage between the Turks & Caicos Banks to migrate to and from their breeding grounds in the Caribbean. Scuba divers often hear their characteristic calls over the winter months, with sail boats providing the best opportunities to observe them on the surface, though a discrete distance must always be maintained to ensure that they are not disturbed.

Old~world Charm

The salt raking days may be long gone, but the island of Grand Turk still displays many reminders of those pioneering times. Besides over 200 acres of salinas, much of the local architecture reveals further Bermudian influence, from the charming public buildings to the grand historic homes. Wooden constructions prevail, since the tall ships that once exported the salt brought with them skilled carpenters and a good supply of timber. Local sources were also once available, with tree felling being encouraged to limit rainfall, thereby helping salt production, and driftwood often being washed ashore from the ships wrecked on the treacherous fringing reefs. Many of the houses display the classic wide verandas, wooden-slatted louvers and fancy trellis work, which are not only aesthetically pleasing, but more importantly help to cool the interior, easing life in a tropical climate. Likewise, their pastel painted exteriors create a rainbow of colour that complements the rich hues of the trailing Bougainvillaea

and helps to reflect the heat in this land of perpetual sunshine. The roofs are also designed with the climate in mind, their characteristic steep pitch and lack of eaves reducing their chances of being prised off in the event of a hurricane. But, apart from these rare violent storms, very little rain now reaches this island, and the roofs also serve as large catchment areas to collect the precious freshwater when it eventually does arrive.

The people that live on Grand Turk, together with all the other islanders, have strong Christian beliefs that have seen them through both troubled and good times and will no doubt continue to guide them in the future. Like their houses, the churches they frequent are mostly of Bermudian style and often tower above the landscape, their grand spires and beautiful stained-glass windows an inspiring sight for all. Full every Sunday, they sway to the rhythm of the congregation, with traditional hymns being sung alongside gospel music, in scenes that have probably changed little since emancipation. Today, many of the other historic buildings in Cockburn Town, the nation's capital, have been lovingly restored to their former grandeur and once again stand proud to receive their guests. Both the Turks Head Hotel and the Salt Raker Inn are impressive wooden buildings overlooking the sea that date back to the mid nineteenth century.

Guinep Lodge, with its wonderful Bermudian architecture, must be the perfect setting for the Turks & Caicos National Museum. Here, the varied history of the islands is brought to life, with exhibits including discoveries from both land and marine archaeological sites. Other historical artefacts are readily seen around Grand Turk, such as this bronze cannon that stands outside the Governor's Residence.

The colonial mansion of the Turks Head Hotel boasts an auspicious past. Built in the mid-nineteenth century, it was once the Governor's private guesthouse, later becoming the American Consulate and then finally a small hotel. Just down the road, another historic retreat is located behind a white walled garden, where the Salt Raker Inn, a former Bermudian shipwright's house, provides a popular watering hole for locals and visitors alike.

Overlooking Red Salina near the centre of Cockburn Town, the architectural style of the Grand Turk Methodist Church suggests a much older origin than the building's 1930 construction date. However, the Methodist congregation was established in the islands over a century before this and the present landmark was erected on the site of the original church, which was destroyed in the hurricane of 1926.

Also, the splendid modern exhibits of the National Museum are housed in Guinep Lodge, a beautiful setting that is complemented by the adjacent garden, where displays of native and introduced plants grow side by side. Newer constructions nestle among those with stories to tell, but frequently go unnoticed as their architects have unashamedly copied the tried and tested designs of old. Often, behind these historic facades, lies a very different world of modern computers and telecommunications. Holding tax free status and being situated on the doorstep of the Americas, the Turks & Caicos have been able to develop a thriving offshore finance industry, which is responsible for enticing thousands of foreign investors here each year.

Although the locals may today enjoy the benefits of a tax haven, their ancestors were not so fortunate. In fact, it was the taxes once levied on the prosperous industries of the past that have indirectly shaped the more recent history of these islands. As the salt industry grew, so did Bahamian interest in the economy and by 1771 the Bermudian salt rakers found themselves being heavily taxed on their valuable exports. Since little of the revenue generated

Saint George's Parish
Church on South Caicos is
one of the island's oldest buildings,
though the delightful stained-glass windows
are more recent additions. Outside, Common
Ground Doves *(Columbina passerina)* flit among the
gravestones and well tended shrubs, extending the peaceful
ambience of the church through their symbolism. These
little birds are nearly always seen in pairs, searching the
ground for seeds while softly cooing to one another.

was seen to benefit the salt islands, the feud that developed between the settlers and the House of Assembly in Nassau was perhaps inevitable. Formal federation with the Bahamas lasted less than fifty years, largely because of the continual protests to the British government by the disgruntled islanders. Eventually, in 1848, an Act was passed that allowed these 'Out Islands' to be governed internally from Grand Turk under a Presidency, but this auspicious arrangement also proved to be relatively short-lived. When a devastating hurricane struck in 1866, hundreds of homes were destroyed and over a million bushels of salt were washed away, causing the country's economy to collapse overnight.

Needing a helping hand to recover financially, the islanders turned to Jamaica, a British Colony that was then riding high on a wave of prosperity. The subsequent Jamaican rule of the Turks & Caicos lasted from 1873 until Jamaica's independence eighty-nine years later, but this proved no more fruitful for the Turks Islanders than their previous affiliation. Thus, in 1962 these islands became a separate British dependency, a status they retain to this day. While this move was welcomed by the locals, who wanted a greater say in their home affairs, it took a further fourteen years before constitutional reforms allowed this Crown Colony to be governed by an Executive Council elected by the people.

Clearly, throughout their political history the Turks & Caicos have retained strong ties with Britain, though increasingly their American neighbours are influencing the nation's future. Following the recall of Jamaican currency in 1973, the islands' legal tender became the U.S. dollar and much of the recent development has stemmed from the United States and Canada. Today, with most imports originating out of Florida and satellite dishes receiving American television networks, it is perhaps not surprising that the younger generation in particular have a closer affinity to America than with Old Blighty 3000 miles away. Nevertheless, wandering through the narrow streets of Cockburn Town, scenes reminiscent of times gone by repeatedly confront the newcomer. In amongst the picturesque colonial-style buildings,

In terms of local government, the seat of power rests in Grand Turk, with Cockburn Town being the capital of this island nation. Originally, all government offices were located here on Front Street, but now many have been moved further south to the former US Air Force base near the Governor's Residence of Waterloo. The iron cannons that guard the legislative buildings probably came from the wreck of HMS Endymion, which foundered on the reefs south of Salt Cay in 1790.

women sit on white stone walls braiding hair, peels of laughter come from beneath a Tamarind tree where a group of men compete in a friendly game of 'bones' (dominoes) and gleeful children can be seen in the distance fishing and diving off an old wooden dock. No soaring tower blocks break the horizon, no billboards bombard the passer-by with unwanted hype and even

With a much closer proximity to mainland America than the British Isles, the United States undoubtedly has a greater influence on the islands, especially the youth. However, the strong national pride that seems instilled within all local people helps to maintain the unique identity of the Turks & Caicos. As with the past, the key to the future may lie within the Coat of Arms, which depicts the islands' wonderful natural resources that visitors now come to see.

the roads seem devoid of motorised traffic, functioning more like pavements, cycle tracks and bridle paths than busy highways.

If time appears to have moved slowly on Grand Turk then it must have really stood still on the neighbouring island of Salt Cay. As its name suggests, this was once the nucleus of the salt industry and seems to have changed little since the Bermudians first settled here centuries ago. The peaceful landscape that surrounds the only settlement, Balfour Town, is still dominated by the shallow salt pans that today lie undisturbed, forming rich feeding grounds for native and migratory waterfowl. Here, spindly windmills break the skyline, their now idle vanes serving only as convenient perches for Ospreys, Brown Pelicans and assorted herons. Meanwhile, feral donkeys roam the low-walled roads amidst a riot of tropical colour that cascades from the adjacent flower gardens and fills the air with the sweet perfume of Frangipani. As with the other salt islands, the houses are also reminiscent of past times, from the humble cottages that make up the town to the imposing White House, the island's first stone building. Having remained virtually unaffected by the rapid social changes that have occurred elsewhere in the island chain, Salt Cay is a living memorial to the country's rich cultural heritage.

Bones, or dominoes, is a popular local pastime with four players, plus spectators, often seen huddled around a small table, positioned under the canopy of a shady tree. Everyone seems to know all the possible combinations and a key piece is invariably produced with a flourish, then slammed down onto the playing surface with a loud bang. Here, a rather amusing forfeit for the current loser has been devised, putting an edge on a friendly competition.

Unlike Grand Turk, Salt Cay hides no secrets beneath its old-world charm. Since the demise of the salt industry, many have left to seek employment, leaving behind a bastille for the very young and elderly. For the lucky visitors who come here though, Salt Cay offers pure escapism in beautiful surroundings and a warm sense of belonging generated by the local community. Consequently, tourism is beginning to touch this idyllic location, but at such a low level as to exert only a positive influence. A small dive operation and a few guesthouses have provided much-needed jobs and the legacies of the salt trade are currently undergoing a facelift. For many years now, the National Trust has been dedicated to preserving the natural and cultural heritage of the Turks & Caicos and one of their many projects is the restoration of selected historic ruins on Salt Cay. Besides creating mere tourist attractions, it is also important to maintain these links to the past so that future generations of islanders can recognise what makes their wonderful culture so unique.

You are more likely to meet a donkey on the well-kept streets of Salt Cay than any form of motorised transport. Descended from the animals that hauled salt carts, they now take life at a leisurely pace, like the rest of the island. Generally people get about Balfour Town on foot or by bicycle and besides scuba diving, this is probably the most energetic thing visitors have to do, though exploring the island is well worth the effort.

Undoubtedly, as tourism develops further on Grand Turk, so will the number of planes that make the five-minute flight to this sleepy little cay, bringing tourists keen to experience the tranquillity and hospitality of such a peerless hideaway. However, as with the visitors, the locals love Salt Cay just the way it is and so few changes are likely to occur in the foreseeable future.

Remnants of the former salt industry, such as the salinas, windmills and sluice gates, still dominate the Salt Cay landscape. Today, some 150 years since it was built by Bermudian settlers, the White House remains arguably the most imposing building. It was constructed from imported stones previously used as ballast, with the living quarters on the first floor. The lower area was used as a store for the salt.

The Tide of Change

Today, Providenciales may well be considered the pearl within the necklace of islands that decorates the Caicos Bank, but more gems are currently in the making. With different developers each wanting their own slice of paradise, the other main islands and cays have all received considerable interest over recent years and tourism looks set to spread quickly throughout the nation. To date, the small cays that are strung between Provo and North Caicos have received the most attention, with several development projects already underway, or completed. The highly exclusive destinations of Pine Cay and Parrot Cay build on the existing infrastructure and reputation of Provo and are within easy access of its international airport, yet still offer total seclusion to their rich and famous clientele. Meanwhile, other developers have been even more ambitious, looking further afield to create their own luxurious resorts.

The private purchase of Big Ambergris Cay clearly shows how tourism development is now reaching even the remote areas of the archipelago. This rocky outpost is situated on the south-eastern edge of the Caicos Bank and probably represents the most isolated habitable land, being over thirty miles from Grand Turk and fifty miles from Provo. The cay was named after a waxy substance that occasionally washes ashore on the east-facing beaches and originates as a secretion in the gut of Sperm Whales. When fresh, ambergris is black, greasy and has a rather unpleasant smell, but if left to dry in the sun, or diluted with solvents, it develops quite a pleasant aroma. In the past it was highly valued, partially for its alleged medicinal properties, but mainly by the perfumery trade, which still use this natural substance today. The quantities found on Big Ambergris Cay were once enough to support a small settlement, but, perhaps as a result of the whaling trade, the supply was soon exhausted and the settlers subsequently moved on. Ever since, this and the neighbouring cays have served as havens for wildlife, being visited only by fishermen keen to exploit the riches of their coral reefs. However, with the large-scale trans-formations proposed by the new owners, many more visitors are destined to arrive in the future.

Beach front resorts, apartment villas and luxury holiday homes are popping up all along the north coast of Providenciales and other islands are sure to follow suit, though all developments are being strictly regulated. Although tourism may represent the future of the Turks & Caicos, the major emphasis is on maintaining their natural beauty, for this is what the visitors are coming to experience.

History has shown that the rare Turks & Caicos Rock
Iguana *(Cyclura carinata)* has never mixed well with
human settlement, with cats and dogs having exterminated
them on all but the smaller uninhabited islands. The
population on Big Ambergris Cay, however, remains
healthy and as a proviso to the proposed development,
several iguanas are to be relocated to bolster the numbers
on neighbouring cays.

Preserving the natural heritage of the Turks & Caicos, while at the same time meeting economic goals, is one of the biggest challenges for the government. The luxury hotels and condominiums planned for Big Ambergris Cay present special problems since this island is a stronghold for two of the nation's indigenous species, the Rock Iguana and the Turks Head Cactus. Both have come under increasing threat from habitat changes brought about by urban expansion and need long term protection for their continued survival. Therefore, as part of the contractual agreement on the sale of this land, a large acreage must remain in its untamed state to serve as a sanctuary for the native wildlife.

Without doubt, the greatest source of change that is likely to hit this nation in the next few years is the proposed East Caicos development. Although currently the largest uninhabited island in the Greater Caribbean, it may soon become home to a huge purpose-built cruise liner port, along with all the associated tourist amenities. In a truly ambitious multi-million dollar engineering enterprise, a massive berthing facility is to be excavated from the heart of the island, to include a turning circle and docks capable of accommodating up to twelve modern-day cruise liners. By upgrading the existing airport on South Caicos, it is intended that all airfreight will reach the development via a linking road that will bridge the two islands, spanning the

Large areas of Big Ambergris Cay are covered with Turks Head Cacti *(Melocactus intortus)* including several plots marked for development. But their significance as a national emblem means these plants cannot be destroyed and must be replanted nearby to maintain the local population. Like the corals that form the reef, these cacti are slow growing and take up to ten years to reach maturity. Their numbers often require decades to recover from disturbances.

Atlantic rollers crash onto the rocky tip of East Caicos as
they have surely done since the limestone first rose from
the waves. This low-lying tropical real estate is currently the
largest uninhabited island in the Greater Caribbean, being
over ten miles long and hosting some fantastic beaches on
its northern shore. Its development is perhaps inevitable,
though the proposed scale may be surprising.

narrow channels that exist between them. Also, among the plans is the proposal to extend this road across to Middle and North Caicos, eventually linking South Caicos to Providenciales in an inter-archipelago highway, much like the one that exists in the Florida Keys.

The scale of the proposed development is such that it will almost certainly establish the Turks & Caicos as one of the premier cruise destinations in the Greater Caribbean. However, the environmental and socio-economic considerations for such a project are immense. Towards the north of the island, a ridge of relatively high land occurs that is skirted by wonderful beaches, but the rest of East Caicos is mainly composed of salt marshes, swamps and mudflats. Although this area may not seem too hospitable to us and therefore, perhaps well suited for developing, the habitat is highly significant for birdlife and is a vital nursery area for marine species. Indeed, in recognition of its status, the north-western end of the island along with the vast majority of Middle Caicos and a large proportion of North Caicos were designated a Ramsar Site in 1990. This international treaty was established to safeguard wetlands of global importance and consequently almost 135 000 acres of the Turks & Caicos

Mangroves and swampy areas may seem like wastelands, with their thick mud and eager mosquitoes, but they act as vital feeding sites for birds and other animals. The Tricoloured Heron *(Hydranassa tricolor)* is often seen wading the secluded waters in search of fish, while the Belted Kingfisher *(Ceryle alcyon)* will dive-bomb for its supper. The fact that people are less likely to disturb these watery retreats can make them a refuge worth preserving.

are currently protected. With the location of the proposed development being adjacent to such sensitive ecosystems, concerns have been raised as to the effects the construction and subsequent influx of people will have on the local wildlife.

To be weighed against any potential environmental impact is the boost this port would give to the local economy, as well as the promise of creating nearly 7000 jobs. This is likely to be a great incentive for the repatriation of many Turks Islanders, who have previously left to seek employment in the Bahamas, Jamaica or America. As a result, the population may snowball, with locals returning for new work opportunities and each day thousands of sea-borne tourists arriving, eager to indulge in this tropical wonderland. However, concomitant with this economic growth is the potential loss of the small fishing and farming communities of the central Caicos Islands, which will have to struggle to survive amidst the inevitable social changes that will sweep the nation. It can only be hoped that their traditional skills and customs continue to be passed down through the generations and that their unique character and culture will be retained.

Riding a donkey is one way of getting around North Caicos, especially when collecting the fruits of the Tamarind tree *(Tamarindus indica)*. Although common on most of the islands, the tree has been introduced, its name deriving from the Arabic *tamr hindi*, meaning 'date of India'. The pods contain an acidic pulp with an exceptionally high sugar content, giving this fruit a popular but rather acquired taste.

Prickly Pear cacti *(Opuntia dillenii)* are abundant throughout
the islands, where they have been harvested since the days
of the Taino Indians. Besides their edible red fruits, the
flower buds can be cooked as a vegetable and their swollen
stems used to make a medicinal tea. Here, a local
Rastafarian carefully prepares the pads, as de-spined and
split open they are an excellent hair conditioner.

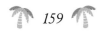

Children are the lifeblood of any nation and this is certainly recognised within the Turks & Caicos. Both boys and girls are always immaculately dressed, with the girls having intricately braided hair that represents hours of grooming and portrays a pride in themselves, as well as their community. Events like this National Youth Day on South Caicos are often staged, harnessing their boundless energy and enthusiasm while providing them with a sense of their national heritage.

Small communities the world over face the problem of their young folk departing in search of employment and this exodus is often cause for concern. In the past, there has been a steady flow of youngsters towards Providenciales and sometimes abroad, but these displaced locals always seem to maintain a strong sense of their original island identity. With the spread of tourism and the work opportunities it provides, many are now returning to settle in their home islands for good.

As the future of the Turks & Caicos is poised for change yet again, it is important now more than ever to protect the natural splendours, as these are the features that most of the new visitors will be coming to see. With nature hanging in the balance, it is imperative that the proposed developments have minimal effect on both the terrestrial and marine environments. Through human intervention, the Caribbean Monk Seal and Manatees have already been lost from the surrounding seas and the brightly coloured Bahama Parrots are absent from the local treetops. It would be a bleak winter indeed if the song of the Humpback Whale no longer echoed through the water and flocks of flamingos failed to light up the sky with their majestic beauty.

One island that has witnessed many fluctuations in its prosperity is South Caicos, or the 'Big South' as it is affectionately known to the locals. There have already been a couple of attempts at tourist development here, but unfortunately the abandoned hotel shells on East Bay serve as a regular reminder to the local community of broken promises and lost opportunities. However, the future looks more promising, with the development of a new hotel complex on High Point, which looks set to revive the struggling, fishing-based economy of the island. Located near Two Sister's Hill, the highest vantage point on South Caicos, this

Fringed Filefish (*Monacanthus ciliatus*) are generally brown or green, as their time is spent hidden amongst seagrass fronds, or drifting with clumps of algae. However, this juvenile is unusually pale, having camouflaged itself against a floating piece of white plastic. With an ever-increasing number of tourists, the people of the Turks & Caicos will have to be extra vigilant to safeguard their natural paradise.

The old District Commissioner's Residence on South
Caicos is a rather stately building that rests on a rocky
promontory overlooking the town of Cockburn Harbour.
A sign of the changing times, it has now been converted to
a quaint guesthouse, where visitors are treated to
breathtaking panoramic views of the town, harbour, nearby
cays and the adjacent fringing reef of East Bay.

establishment will provide impressive views of the rollers washing onto the shore of Long Beach to the east and the serene turquoise waters of Bell Sound to the west.

For the locals of South Caicos there's a deep-rooted belief that the town receives little rain because heat radiates from the nearby salinas causing the passing clouds to part. Just like the clouds that come so close and then move on, the people of South Caicos have had their economic hopes raised on several occasions, only to have them fade again as natural resources become no longer viable, or developers pull out. Eventually the rain does fall, however, and with it comes a transformation, relieving hardships and rejuvenating the arid land. Nevertheless, clouds can also turn into thunderstorms and, likewise, economic benefits can bring with them their own inherent risks. If the Cruise Liner Port is developed on East Caicos and the two islands linked by road, this will undoubtedly bring financial salvation to many families and South Caicos will truly become the Big South again. But, as another tide of change rolls over these islands, let us hope that the land and its people remain forever 'Beautiful by Nature'.

Crew members aboard this beached yacht have unfurled a tarpaulin that more frequently provides shade, but which now offers shelter from an incoming squall. The land may be invigorated by this splash of freshwater, though its power to dissolve limestone may weaken the rock. So too may tourism represent a double-edged sword, with developers needing to protect the environment to ensure that the Turks & Caicos people can always have pride in their beautiful islands.

GLOSSARY OF TERMS

Abyssal Of, or relating to, the ocean depths or floor.

Algae A diverse group of chiefly aquatic, photosynthetic organisms, ranging in size from single-celled individuals to large seaweeds (macroalgae). Although they have now been assigned their own taxonomic group, algae are traditionally thought of as plants and have been treated as such for the purposes of this book.

Arawak A large and important language family originating from South America and comprising several tribes, many of which migrated northwards into the West Indies.

Archipelago A group of islands and their adjacent waters.

Belonger Someone who holds a Turks and Caicos passport, but does not necessarily originate from these islands. *see* Turks Islander.

Bryozoans Small, aquatic invertebrates, mainly comprising marine species, that permanently attach to hard surfaces, such as rock and seagrasses, where they form encrusting or branching colonies.

Carib A member of a group of fierce tribes from northern South America and the West Indies, after whom the Caribbean Sea was named.

Cay Pronounced 'key'. A small, low-lying island composed mainly of coral or sand.

Crustaceans A group of animals including lobsters, crabs and shrimps, that are characterised by their segmented body, external skeleton of chitin, paired jointed legs and two pairs of antennae.

Ecosystem A natural system defined by the organisms that live within it and how they interact not only with one another, but also with elements of the non-living environment.

Endemic An organism that is only found in a certain region.

Epiphyte A plant that grows on the surface of another plant to obtain mechanical support, but not to derive nourishment or water.

Fauna The species that make up the animal community in a particular region or period. *see* Flora.

Flora A term that refers to the collective plant species of a particular region or period. *see* Fauna.

Food Chain A series of organisms, usually beginning with plants, in which each member is consumed by the next one in the chain.

Gorgonians A group of plant-like corals, including sea whips and sea fans, with an internal, flexible skeleton of horny material and polyps always bearing eight tentacles. *see* Reef-Building Corals.

Greater Caribbean The region comprising the Caribbean Sea and its associated islands, the Gulf of Mexico and the Bahamas.

Guano The dung of bats or sea-birds that accumulates along certain coastal areas or in caves and is often used as a fertiliser.

Littoral Living on the seashore, especially in the area subjected to tidal emersion.

Mangrove A woody, tropical plant with adaptations for living in salty, waterlogged soils, often forming dense thickets along tidal shores.

Molluscs A large, diverse group of soft-bodied invertebrates that often live within protective shells they produce around themselves. Include many popular seafood species, such as clams, squid and conch.

Nematocyst Stinging cells found in corals, sea anemones, hydroids and jellyfish that are discharged either by contact or chemicals and used for capturing prey or for protection.

New World A term used to refer to the Western Hemisphere, including North and South America, and the Caribbean Islands, which was the 'new land' discovered by Columbus.

Pelagic Living in the open water as opposed to the coastal region or near the sea bottom.

Photosynthesis The light-driven process in green plants and certain other organisms by which carbon dioxide and water are used to produce simple sugars, with the subsequent release of oxygen as a by-product.

Plankton The collective term for aquatic organisms that drift with the currents, especially at or near the surface, and form the base of many food chains. Mainly comprising bacteria, algae and small invertebrates, this group also includes jellyfish and fish larvae with weak swimming abilities.

Pneumatophores Spongy, chimney-like structures that grow from the roots of certain mangrove species and project out of the oxygen-poor sediments in order to supply the submerged tissues with the gases they need.

Polyp One of many small, anemone-like individuals that make up a coral colony, having a ring of tentacles around a mouth leading to a shared gut.

Prop Roots The large stilt-like roots of certain mangrove species that arise from the main trunk to form arched supports that barely need to penetrate the soil.

Reef-Building Corals Colonial organisms that contain symbiotic zooxanthellae within their tissues, which serve to promote the production of their skeleton and hence give rise to reef formation. *see* Gorgonians.

Rhizomes The horizontal 'runners' of seagrasses and other plants that send out shoots above and roots below and help to consolidate the shifting sediments through the latticework they create.

Salina A shallow sea-water pond, which in tropical regions may have been cleared of vegetation and used for the commercial production of salt.

Substratum The base to which a sedentary animal or plant is attached (plural substrata).

Symbiosis A close, often obligatory association between two organisms of different species in which either or both members may derive some benefit.

Taino A member of a peaceful Arawak tribe that inhabited the Greater Antilles and Bahamas chain, but who were annihilated by the Spanish during the 16th century. *see* Arawak.

Turks Islander Someone who is born in the Turks and Caicos Islands. *see* Belonger.

Xerophyte A plant adapted to dry and desert conditions, often possessing swollen water-storing stems or leaves.

Zooxanthellae Single-celled algae that live within the tissues of reef-building corals, giving them their coloration and promoting the formation of the coral's skeleton.

ACKNOWLEDGMENTS

We would like to extend our sincere gratitude to the many people and organisations who assisted us in producing this book. In particular, we are most appreciative of the times that Cornelius Basden, Mae Clarke, Cindy Grotsky, Christie Hall, Brian Riggs and Ossie Virgil spent with us during our stay on the islands, and for the local knowledge they imparted. For giving us some wonderful opportunities to obtain photographs we must thank the Department of the Environment and Coastal Resources, 'Ganger', Eric Zigas, Paul Leonard, Don and Suzanne McCormick, Broadreach Inc., the organisers of the TCI Billfish tournament, and the various dive operators listed opposite. The other logos shown are mainly of TCI companies that supported our venture through providing us with accommodation or transportation on the islands, to whom we are also indebted. We would especially like to thank Mrs Taylor from Middle Caicos, Clifford Gardiner, Alan Tatham, Edward Clotworthy, Vernon Ellis and Harold Charles. Also, Alan James from 'Current State Diving' in the UK kindly loaned us an underwater strobe for our return visit to the islands, which was much appreciated.

While the views expressed in the book are our own, we obtained the information presented from many reputable sources, though assume full responsibility for any inaccuracies that may be present. Brian Riggs helped us considerably with the historical aspects of the islands, as did the museum exhibits and the published work of the late Herbert Sadler. Ethylin Gibbs-Williams and Dean Bernal were generous with their time and knowledge of the local environmental issues, and we wish both their charitable organisations, The National Trust and the Jo Jo Project, continued success in the future. On this note we must also thank Dean for supplying the photograph from the Jo Jo Archives that appears on page 140 of this book. Several botanists came to our rescue in identifying the local flora, in particular Sean Carrington, Charles Dills, Derek Butcher, Eric Gouda and Kenneth Quinn. We would also like to thank Gary Morgan, Don Buden and Barbara French, who provided us with research information about the resident bat and snake species, and Piotr Naskrecki for his entomological expertise.

For their editorial contributions, we are extremely grateful to Kathy Borsuk, Keith Martin-Smith, and Derek and Sherry-Ann Carrington. Our families deserve a special mention for both their collective comments regarding the manuscript and for their continued encouragement and enthusiasm for this project. We must also thank Liquid Engineering UK Ltd for providing office facilities in our time of need. Also, Kathy Lowe and Sally House gave valuable suggestions concerning the book layout, which were most appreciated.

Finally, we would like to give special thanks to all the islanders, especially the children of South Caicos, who made our time in the Turks and Caicos so enjoyable.

Art Pickering's

TCI Tel: 1 • 649 • 946 • 4232
Fax: 1 • 649 • 941 • 5296
P.O. Box 219, Providenciales
US Tel: 1 • 800 • 833 • 1341
em provoturtledivers@provo.net
www.provoturtledivers.com

JoJo Dolphin Project

TCI Tel/Fax: 1 • 649 • 941 • 5617
P.O. Box 153, Providenciales
US 1602 Alton Rd, P.O. Box 599,
Miami Beach, Florida 33139
em jojo1@tciway.tc
www.jojo.tc

Pelican Beach Hotel

TCI Tel: 1 • 649 • 946 • 7112
Fax: 1 • 649 • 946 • 7139
Whitby, North Caicos
em reservations@tciway.tc

Budget Rent A Car

TCI Tel: 1 • 649 • 946 • 5400
or: 1 • 649 • 946 • 4079
Fax: 1 • 649 • 941 • 5364
P.O. Box 32, Providenciales
US Tel: 1 • 800 • 527 • 0700
em budget@provo.net

Le Deck Hotel

TCI Tel: 1 • 649 • 946 • 5547
Fax: 1 • 649 • 946 • 5770
P.O. Box 144, Providenciales
US Tel: 1 • 800 • 528 • 1905
em ledeck@tciway.tc

Provo Rent A Car

TCI Tel: 1 • 649 • 946 • 4404
or: 1 • 649 • 946 • 5610
Fax: 1 • 649 • 946 • 4993
P.O. Box 137, Providenciales
em rentacar@tciway.tc
rentacar@provo.net

Caicos Adventures

TCI Tel/Fax: 1 • 649 • 941 • 3346
P.O. Box 47, Providenciales
US Tel: 1 • 800 • 513 • 5822
em divucrzy@tciway.tc
www.caicosadventures.tc

National Museum

TCI Tel: 1 • 649 • 946 • 2160
P.O. Box 188,
Guinep House,
Front Street, Grand Turk
em www.tcmuseum.org

Times of the Islands

TCI Tel: 1 • 649 • 946 • 4788
Fax: 1 • 649 • 941 • 3402
P.O. Box 234, Caribbean
Place, Providenciales
em timespub@tciway.tc
www.timespub.tc

Dive Provo

TCI Tel: 1 • 649 • 946 • 5029
Fax: 1 • 649 • 946 • 5936
P.O. Box 350, Providenciales
US Tel: 1 • 800 • 234 • 7768
em diving@diveprovo.com
www.diveprovo.com

National Trust

TCI Tel/Fax: 1 • 649 • 941 • 5710
Mb: 1 • 649 • 231 • 1172
P.O. Box 540,
Butterfield Square,
Providenciales
em tc.nattrust@tciway.tc

Turks Head Hotel

TCI Tel: 1 • 649 • 946 • 2466
Fax: 1 • 649 • 946 • 1716
P.O. Box 58, Grand Turk
em tophotel@grand-turk.com
www.grand-turk.com

Erebus Inn

TCI Tel: 1 • 649 • 946 • 4240
Fax: 1 • 649 • 946 • 4704
P.O. Box 238, Providenciales
US Tel: 1 • 800 • 323 • 5655
em erebus@tciway.tc
www.erebus.tc

Oasis Divers

TCI Tel/Fax: 1 • 649 • 946 • 1128
P.O. Box 137, Grand Turk
US Tel: 1 • 800 • 892 • 3995
Fax: 1 • 770 • 640 • 7461
em oasisdiv@tciway.tc
www.oasisdivers.com

Salt Raker Inn

TCI Tel: 1 • 649 • 946 • 2260
or: 1 • 649 • 946 • 2263
Fax: 1 • 649 • 946 • 2817
P.O. Box 1, Grand Turk
em sraker@tciway.tc

Flamingo Divers

TCI Tel/Fax: 1 • 649 • 946 • 4193
P.O. Box 322, Providenciales
US Tel: 1 • 800 • 204 • 9282
em flamingo@provo.net
www.provo.net/flamingo

Ocean Club

TCI Tel: 1 • 649 • 946 • 5880
Fax: 1 • 649 • 946 • 5845
P.O. Box 240, Providenciales
US Tel: 1 • 800 • 457 • 8787
em oceanclb@tciway.tc
www.ocean-club.com

SkyKing

TCI Tel: 1 • 649 • 941 • 3136
or: 1 • 649 • 946 • 4594
Fax: 1 • 649 • 941 • 5127
P.O. Box 398, Providenciales
em king@tciway.tc
www.skyking.tc

INDEX

Note: Numbers in **bold** refer to pages with illustrations.